THREE FUNERALS
AND A WEDDING

THREE FUNERALS
AND A WEDDING

JOHN THORP

The Book Guild Ltd

First published in Great Britain in 2018 by
The Book Guild Ltd
9 Priory Business Park
Wistow Road, Kibworth
Leicestershire, LE8 0RX
Freephone: 0800 999 2982
www.bookguild.co.uk
Email: info@bookguild.co.uk
Twitter: @bookguild

Typeset in Adobe Garamond Pro

Printed and bound in the UK by CPI Group (UK) Ltd, Croydon, CR0 4YY

ISBN 978 1912362 721

British Library Cataloguing in Publication Data.
A catalogue record for this book is available from the British Library.

'Change is inevitable, except from a vending machine.'
Robert C Gallagher

CONTENTS

ABOUT THE AUTHOR

John Thorp has worked in business for more than 25 years, mainly in IT leadership roles at, amongst others, Laura Ashley, The Burton Group, Compass Group, easyJet and Dixons Stores Group, where, at the last two, he was a member of the management board. He has a Masters degree from Cranfield University, where he was also a visiting lecturer, and has worked in a non-executive and voluntary capacity as well as a paid adviser to several private, public and charitable organisations.

Throughout his career he has been heavily involved in the evaluation and integration of merged and acquired businesses, and through that, major business change.

He is not to be confused with the other John Thorp, author of the *Information Paradox*, and the US expert in value and benefits management in IT projects. They have led similar careers in parts – both have been associated with Cranfield University, and both have extensive public speaking experience on similar issues. The author of this book believes he may have benefitted at least once from the confusion by being asked to speak at a prestigious international conference on business change: he relates that from the favourable reception he got at the time and the positive feedback afterwards, he believes he may have got away with it, but whether this was because he did a good job, or because the mistake was never exposed, remains unclear.

ACKNOWLEDGEMENTS

I would like to thank the numerous people who have contributed towards this book by providing material, checking facts or reviewing my early attempts. They include colleagues, friends and advisers, and without their generously provided time this project would not have been possible. Most of them, for reasons which should be self-evident, have elected to remain anonymous, but you know who you are. For others, who have not explicitly made this a condition of their participation, I have decided they also should remain unnamed, as to identify just a few might mean they attract an unjustifiably high proportion of the blame. You too know who you are, and once again, I offer my sincere thanks.

In recognition of the above, I would like to dedicate this book to them. Over the years, I have worked with many amazing people who have inspired me in my endeavours, steered me along my career and given me the freedom to fail or succeed by my own wits, but mostly, in spite of my own folly, ensured that I did the latter.

INTRODUCTION

This book is about systems and change. It is not about the usual, much-discussed issue of 'business change management' – the hot topic when introducing new Information Technology (IT) systems – it is about fundamentally what change is, how systems in the widest sense of the word cause change, and how the impacts of these changes are often unintentional and can have profound and sometimes catastrophic consequences for the organisations concerned. It is also about how significant change is often introduced into a business without anyone consciously realising it.

It might seem self-evident that introducing new 'IT' is putting in place a new 'system', but it is surprising how many business and IT people choose to ignore even this apparently obvious fact. Indeed, both parties have their own reasons to be in denial: people hate change, they are used to and often expert in working the way they've always done; their current knowledge has led to them being valued, perhaps to recognition and reward, maybe just to an easy life. Change disrupts all that. When asked by naive IT people what they want from a new system, business people often say *what I have now – it must do what this one does*. It then takes a brave, visionary, confident, and equally (or more) knowledgeable IT person to say, *'no – this will be different, better, it will improve the organisation. If you just want what you have now, then, I'll tell you what, keep it and we'll save the money'.* However, most IT people don't do that: they want to put in new systems – that's what they like doing after all. If an organisation is fortunate and has people with the right experience and approach, they will be good at it; most will not.

It is easy to underestimate the impact of a new system of any kind: IT in particular 'hard-wires' a part, or sometimes all, of an organisation in a way which can be very difficult to subsequently unpick. As we shall see, once that system is in place, it conditions how things will be done. These things may be the right ones, or they may be wrong; they might have been deliberately designed (by people who believed at the time – but, again, were possibly mistaken – that it was the right way) or, more commonly, they might have been accidentally introduced.

The problem though is that it's not just IT: then it should be easy to know when a new 'system' is coming; with other kinds of change, it's not. Whenever you change an organisation's structure, put in place a new incentive scheme, acquire or merge with another business, or sometimes make what appears to be the simplest adjustment to a minor process, you are initiating change. You are putting in place a new system, whether you know it or not.

The impact of that can be wide-ranging, and unless the new system is explicitly designed to produce precisely the outputs you want, you will, with 100% certainty, get precisely the ones you don't.

This then is the story of four businesses. The only link between them is that I happened to work for them all at a time when they were embarking on a period of enormous change. My involvement, as with the fact that I worked for these companies at all, was largely accidental. Although my contribution may have been small, I was deeply involved with what was taking place, and in every case it was a fascinating experience – an education in how to affect change, or how not to, and a masterclass in leadership and vision, or lack of it. Looking back, I now see that it gave me a unique insider's view which was to inform and shape my career for 25 years.

All businesses which have expanded rapidly have faced similar challenges: how to keep hold of the core ethos which created the business in the first place; how to recruit new people, develop current leaders, and build teams which share that ethos; how to increase sales while retaining profitability; and at the same time, how not to lose control.

All businesses need to change – this is a truism which has been endlessly written about – and growth is a particularly dangerous thing. There are many drivers: increasing customer demand; potential in new markets; the necessity to achieve 'scale' (often quoted, but rarely defined); pressure from shareholders for greater returns (particularly true for publically owned companies); but equally often, simply vanity and ambition in the boardroom.

Much has been written on what to do and how to go about it, from the marvellous *E-Myth* by Michael E. Gerber[1] (written in 1986, ironically at the time of the first case study here and never out of print or out of date since), to the wisdom of the great theorists such as Peter Drucker and

Michael Porter, and the visionary practitioners such as Jack Welsh, Lou Gerstner and Anne Mulcahy.

The lesson from all of these is simple – get it right and you will survive and prosper: get it wrong and you will die.

The one thing they all agree on is that ultimately you have no choice – as Jack Welsh said:

'Control your own destiny, or someone else will.' [2]

These stories are of four businesses faced with this challenge, what they did and what the outcome was. They are all still around today, albeit in some instances in very different forms; but in some cases, they very nearly weren't.

They are based on my personal experiences at the time and reflections since, but they are presented not merely as uncorroborated anecdotes – they include insights from other people involved, documented evidence from the time and since, and in all cases are hopefully laid out with a clarity only really available to those fortunate enough to benefit from 20/20 hindsight.

They all take the same form: the story as it appeared to me at the time; a discussion of the consequences and of the wider context; and finally, lessons and conclusions which I and others drew from the experience.

Notes

Each chapter has a collection of Endnotes, to be found at the back of the book. These are a mixture of formal references and acknowledgements, ideas for further reading, and random thoughts, anecdotes and asides which didn't seem to quite fit into the main body. They should be read in conjunction with the text, or ignored, as the reader sees fit.[3]

LA STORY

1

Early 1986 was an interesting time for Laura Ashley. Now an international household name, back then it had a niche but well-established market in the UK, and a fanatically loyal customer base who could not get enough of the gentle, past-times nostalgia for floral prints on traditional fabrics. The home furnishings were in demand in every Kensington living room, and the pretty dresses and Victorian-style blouses a must for every self-respecting Chelsea mother and daughter. The Ashleys had successfully converted their Bohemian London roots to a more rural country image with a move to mid-Wales in the late 60s (albeit leaving their design office and retail headquarters in the far more convenient South-East), and business was booming.

Unfortunately, it was also a time of great tragedy. On her 60th birthday, Laura herself had fallen down the stairs at her home in Wales and died, and the business (although the impact of this was probably not well enough understood at the time) had lost a figurehead and spiritual leader. Amazingly, this sudden loss did not stop the company going ahead with its much anticipated, 34-times-over-subscribed flotation on the London Stock Exchange two months later, valuing the company at £200 million; the darling of 1980s, Lawson-boom Britain. The company, rudderless, was left under the now unmoderated stewardship of its autocratic and mercurial chairman, Laura's widower, and shortly to be Sir, Bernard Ashley.

To date it had been an amazing success story: profitable and growing in the UK, and starting to explore new markets in Japan, the USA and Europe. The first green lorries had started to appear, proudly bearing the logo '*Laura Ashley: London – Paris – New York*', a far cry from the original kitchen-table printing business in Pimlico.

Much of the expansion had been achieved by doing what they'd always been doing, but harder. Promotion had been internal – someone who a few years before had been a sheep farmer, then lorry driver, had become Director of Distribution; his wife was a warehouse manager; Bernard himself, from a background in the City, but with little experience of running what was now an international business, was Chairman.

This was the company I joined in February 1986 as a wet-behind-the-ears, raring-to-go computer programmer, and was immediately put to work on the most exciting thing a programmer can do: writing a new system. This was to be the software which would run the new flagship warehousing and distribution centre being built in Newtown, Powys, not

4

far from the mid-Wales HQ in Carno. Nowadays, no-one would dream of writing such a thing; any sensible company would buy one pre-formed off the shelf, install it by making the business conform to its proven processes and procedures, and concentrate on what it knows best.

In 1986, however, that probably wasn't an option, and it certainly didn't fit into the prevailing management philosophy of 'we do everything ourselves'. Laura Ashley PLC had thoroughly bought into its own pre-flotation storyline of the ultimate benefits of 'vertical integration', a fashionable buzzword in 1970s and 80s business management schools.[4] A prevailing joke at the time (at least in the sheep-farming valleys of mid-Wales) was that the 'lead-time' for woollen products at Laura Ashley was so named because it started with the ram being 'led' to the ewes.

Times were a-changing, however, and new experts in management consultancy (largely internal and self-appointed) were about to bring new theories and their newly-discovered collective wisdom to bear.

If there is one principle in management consultancy, and one which has kept very many consultants profitably remunerated over the years, it is this:

'If you are centralised, you need to decentralise; if you are decentralised, to centralise.'

Applied to Laura Ashley, a single monolithic company, this was presented as 'break up this tightly integrated business into separate Strategic Business Units (SBUs)', and with that brief, Laura Ashley was plunged into a whole new world of

East Coast US management theory,[5] three-letter acronyms and unbelievable turmoil.

What before were simply the different operating departments of a single, working (if not very well run) company, overnight became separate 'businesses', with the need for their own management boards, operating models, and fatally, profit and loss accounts.[6]

Fundamental questions were raised (if not really addressed); the answers being implicitly embedded in the phrasing:

- What was LA's 'core business': what were its core competencies?
- Where did the value really lie?
- Was it a Retailer? a Manufacturer? maybe that newly emerged concept, a 'Brand'?

There was probably some sensible logic behind these questions, from which might perhaps have come some useful insights on how to scale effectively and not lose sight of the important things. After all, if an operation wasn't 'core' maybe it could be run better as an arms-length entity, outsourced, or even sold for real money to someone else who could run it better and deliver those non-core services back to Laura Ashley. Both manufacturing and distribution could surely be candidates for this approach.

For the thorny question of how to scale and run a retail operation outside the UK (a challenge which, as we shall discuss in more detail later, has taxed and ultimately defeated many a successful UK retailer over the years), maybe a franchise model would make more sense: empower local management with a set of powerful brand tools and 'sell' them product and a brand licence to delegate the risk and retain the profits in the UK.

Even Product Design, the previous holy grail of the business, now that Laura, the inspirational leader of that function, had died, maybe that could be somehow managed internally but 'bought in'. Pursuing this to its logical conclusion, as only management consultants can, maybe the only thing really worth keeping and managing internally was 'The Brand'. To that end, the ultimate SBU was created, the 'Brand Management Group', known, of course, simply as BMG.

As management theories ran wild, so did the excitement and bank-balance-swelling predictions of the effect all this would have on what was now a publically traded stock. Incentive plans were put in place to drive what were determined to be the right outcomes (and here the benefit of that 20/20 hindsight is being fully exploited), and the focus shifted from the external customer and what they might actually want, to that dreaded spectre which came to haunt so many companies at the time, that of the 'internal' customer.

Nothing better illustrates the effect of all this than how it appeared to me in my now highly critical role of guru and font-of-all-knowledge for the newly operational Distribution and Warehousing System (known, of course, simply as DWS). The newly created Distribution division, replete with its own newly appointed Managing Director and Board, decided that the best way to serve its new overseas 'customer' (the newly created European retail division), was by building a huge warehouse in mainland Europe, and leveraging its core assets to run it, namely the systems and technology they had built.

This was nirvana to me. Having spent two years writing and implementing the system in the UK, I was now dispatched to southern Holland as part of the new warehouse team, to be responsible for installing, commissioning and delivering a working system. I was a god in my own kingdom – all-knowing, all-powerful, and utterly indispensable. It was terrifying.

For me, it also provided the first heady taste of working abroad; and of what we all now think of as business change management (the role was only partly technical, involving as it did warehouse design and configuration, process design, set up and training); of being a core part of a large change project; and of the (as it appears to outsiders) prestige and glamour of being an international jet-setter. Or (in the case of my weekly trips to Eindhoven, and the soon-discovered ability to cheaply acquire and need to easily repatriate cases of Grolsch and Amstel) an international North Sea Ferries-setter.

For me it was thrilling; for Laura Ashley it was disastrous. I only realised what was happening, and the consequences for the company of the decisions which had been taken much later, but the defining moment for me was the day the warehouse was finally opened. After the building and now working systems had been handed over to local management, after the tape had been cut and the party had finished, I said goodbye to the team, packed up my things for the last time, and loaded them into the car around the final cases of Grolsch. As I set out onto the motorway and headed north towards the ferry in Rotterdam, I was amazed to see, coming the other way, a seemingly endless procession of Laura Ashley green lorries, *London – Paris – New York* written proudly on the side, heading towards the hitherto empty Weldhoven warehouse.

I was even more amazed when I returned the following month for a (this time) flying visit to see how things were going. The vast warehouse, which we had left just a few weeks before fully configured, but echoing and empty, was now packed to the rafters – every one of our new racks stuffed with rolls and rolls of fabric in every colourway Laura Ashley printed.

Was there really such a huge demand in mainland Europe for this fledgling (for them) business, which depended so much for its success at home on the very English nostalgia for the (English) good-old days, for Victorian values and chintzy floral prints? Had Europe got that?

It took me some time to realise that the question was irrelevant, and incidental to why the warehouse was full. The real reason was much simpler. The Managing Director of European Retail knew a good deal when he saw one (represented in this case by an unbelievably low cost price for the product set by the Fabric Manufacturing Division to generate sales and meet their own targets), and had cornered the market for cotton prints and bought the lot.

Despite there being almost no market yet in Europe for this volume of fabric, he was happy; Manufacturing were happy (and were planning to expand to meet the new demand); and Distribution had had a bumper quarter (and were getting quotes for more lorries). All the incentives triggered pay-outs, and the strategy to divide the company into such obviously high-performing Strategic Business Units looked to be working perfectly.

The only problem was that no-one had thought to consider what was really happening.

And what was happening was that the company was taking itself to the very edge of a very high cliff, over which it subsequently fell.

2

That fall, and subsequent failure to rise, of Laura Ashley PLC has been documented in numerous articles and case studies over the years.

From 1988 until its rescue from bankruptcy by the business conglomerate Malayan United Industries (MUI) 10 years later, Laura Ashley had seven different CEOs (and 11 over 14 years in total). Indeed, during that time the life expectancy of Laura Ashley CEOs shortened every year, from John James who was CEO from 1976 to 1990; Jim Maxmin[7] from 1991 to 1993; Alphonse Schouten[8] from 1993 to 1995 acting as CEO reporting to interim executive chairman, Blakeway Webb;[9] Ann Iverson from 1995 to 1997;[10] David Hoare from 1997 to 1998; and finally Victoria Egan, who lasted a mere five months.

None stayed long enough to bring about any lasting improvement in the company's fortunes, and several arguably contributed to its further decline. Disastrous and expensive adventures in the USA (after huge investment, the business was finally sold to its management for $1 in 1999, along with a write-off by its ex-parent of $34.4 million of debt), plus a move to develop large out-of-town stores in the UK did nothing to improve the finances of anyone other than those executives, who were paid extraordinary amounts for their times in office and often, it seems, even more to vacate them. During this time, the company also flirted with new products – menswear, modern women's business wear, teenage fashion – but nothing seemed to work.

Perhaps the most incredible appointment to the board during this time was that of US TV evangelist, Pat Robertson. An ultra right-wing Republican and former US presidential candidate, Robertson ran the Christian Broadcasting Network, which preached against sexual immorality and homosexuality. As Richard Hyman, an analyst at retail research group Verdict, put it:

'It's clear the owners have decided the only card they can play is the divine intervention card.'[11]

The story of Ann Iverson's remuneration package is particularly illuminating: incentivised to get the share price to £2, she of course did exactly that, triggering a seven-figure bonus and becoming Britain's highest paid businesswoman.[12] When arguably she should have been retrenching the business and focussing on its core operations to clear its debts, she did exactly the opposite, expanding more into large-space outlets in the US and ramping up production in the UK. The collapse in the share price during the period immediately following this peak demonstrated what cost the company, and particularly its misguided investors, had paid for this decision, with 90% wiped from its valuation.

The over-riding part of Ann Iverson's bonus scheme, which was the target of getting the share price to £2, seems incredible today. A more conservative and hard-headed approach to corporate governance, driven by well-publicised mistakes much like this one, have led remuneration committees to set much more balanced targets.[13]

At the time, however, analysts and investors were desperate for a good-news story. As we've become very used to since the internet boom, nothing increases a share price like the optimism generated by a good story, and nothing is better as the basis of a good story than the near-miraculous combination of rapid expansion and increasing profits.

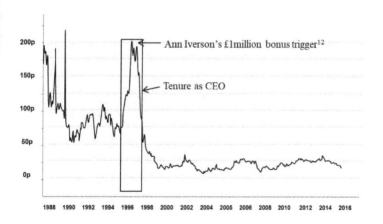

Laura Ashley Historic Share Price 1986-2016

Accounting profits, of course, are a very one-dimensional measure of a company's performance, particularly in a time of rapid growth: cash flow is far more important, and this was becoming hugely negative. Total cash outflow from Laura Ashley from 1990–2000 reached a whopping £250 million, almost all of it provided by fresh cash injections from the new owners, but there were also share issues raising £25 million, plus more than £30 million of debt on the balance sheet from banking facilities. A company valued on flotation at £200 million had been reduced to zero.

Amazingly, throughout all this, and despite only c.16% of the shares being publically traded,[14] LA remained listed on the London Stock Exchange, and the financial humiliation was on full public view for all to watch.

3

I learnt three major lessons from the above sorry story:

Lesson 1: Beware (self-professed) management consultants

Anyone reading the story of the divisionalisation strategy would be perfectly entitled to ask: Who were these management consultants? Who called them in and why? What was their brief? On what were their recommendations based and why was this the conclusion?

They would all be very good questions, both now and, more importantly, at the time. The fact of the matter, from those who were there and recall what happened, is that it is probable they were never asked.

Laura's death, and the sudden conversion into a PLC, brought sharply to the fore what had been driving the company's progress until that time. It could be argued that it had never really had 'management' or a 'strategy' in

15

any formal sense; just the momentum of its own internal energy, and strong design leadership which had succeeded in bringing together a loosely run but ultimately successful company. In the resulting vacuum of poor leadership and a company suddenly having to make difficult decisions about its own future, the self-appointed gurus of management theory found an uncritical and largely unattentive audience.

The speed at which the divisionalisation plan was put into place was staggering, as was the subsequent speed at which the cost base grew. The shift from an external product and customer focus, to an obsession with internal 'customers' and with satisfying a very parochial set of targets, meant that everyone from top to bottom in the organisation took their eye off the ball. The question therefore is how do organisations go about major change, and what role do management consultants (internal or external) play in that?

Internal consultants?

Firstly, the idea of *internal* management consultants, while not unique to this example, is pretty unusual. When we consider how companies select specialists in strategy and business change, high up the list of requirements should be their relative detachment from the current problem under consideration, and their experience: by definition of other companies – ideally of other companies who have faced similar challenges. They should also be steeped in the business of investigating and analysing the problems a company faces both now and in the future, and should bring considerable influencing skills, the ability to encapsulate and communicate complex ideas, and, at least if their own promotional material is to be believed, wisdom.

What role current internal staff can play in this activity is by definition problematic. At one extreme, if they have been with the company for any length of time in positions where they can exercise managerial influence, it would be reasonable to consider them as potentially responsible for, or, at the very least, part of the current state of affairs. Whether they are then able, without considerable external help, to lift themselves above this and consider in a truly objective way what is the best way forward for the company must be debatable. At the other extreme, it is possible that somewhere deep in their psyche is a denial that things need to change: OK, things are not going well, but that isn't because of what I was doing. It would take a highly mature and self-aware person to be able to stand back from that position and propose radical change.

It may be of course that this is just what the newly promoted internal consultants had been waiting for: working for, but not truly engaged with, the company's objectives in the recent past, they now had the chance to prove that the theories which had been dominating their thoughts (maybe to the detriment of that full engagement, and maybe therefore contributing to the downward turn) could be brought to bear to turn it round.

If anything is more dangerous than coming up with half-baked solutions, it is proposing half-baked *pre-formed* ones as the answers to as yet undefined and certainly unanswered questions.

Management consultants

How a company uses management consultants (and as well as employing them and firing them, respecting them and deriding them, I've also worked as one) is a sign of its maturity.

As the old joke goes, a consultant is someone who borrows your watch to tell you the time, and then keeps your watch and sends you the bill for it. There are plenty of others along similar lines, all suggesting that what a management consultant does is charge people a lot of money for delivering something they already knew. And this may be true. It would be rare for a management consultancy assignment to come up with a solution so radical and far-reaching that no-one internally had ever thought of it. It would also be very brave: what consultants aim to do more than anything else is stick around. As someone succinctly put it, the prime objective of a management consultant is to convert a single assignment into an annuity: coming up with a proposal that was so outlandish and new as to be outside the imagination of any of the decision-makers might be a sure way to be shown the door.[15]

On the other hand, the role they can often play very successfully is teasing out from the current management team what might be described as the art of the possible. Having someone external, and someone who is being paid a lot of money to do it, come up with a proposal can often be more acceptable than simply trying to push water uphill internally. That is not to say that they are simply being asked to rubber-stamp (and, in the final reckoning, possibly be blamed for) an unpalatable idea which the CEO wants to implement, such as cost-cutting or relocation (an activity again they are often accused of); it is more likely that the ideas, while existing in some form or another, are embryonic and not yet properly thought through, or there is at the moment no clear way forward in terms of support or implementation plan. Here consultants can not only provide the framework, but also the space for developing these solutions.[16]

All laudable reasons to bring in consultants.

This is not, however, what happened at Laura Ashley. The consultants were all internal, and the speed with which the review proceeded to implementation – less than three months – suggests that the thinking was based more on what was the prevailing management theory than any thoroughgoing analysis of the actual situation.

A consultancy recommendation which focussed simply on organisational change should also have been ringing alarm bells, for two reasons: firstly, no amount of shuffling the parts of a puzzle around is going to lead to a successful outcome unless there is already some pre-existing idea of what it is going to look like when it's finished (i.e. a strategy); and secondly, and more importantly, organisational change as a mechanism for dividing up a company prior to spinning off/selling parts of it might make sense in the longer term, but the effect on the organisation immediately post the new structure did not seem to be considered at all.

As we shall see later, putting in place a new organisation, especially one based so much on arms-length relationships and incentive schemes, is putting in place a powerful new system. And once it is implemented, a system will produce outputs which are generated by its inherent design, not by any (however extreme or well-intentioned) variation of the inputs.

Whole Systems Thinking

More than any other, an organisational system impacts the whole enterprise, and nowhere is it more important to adopt what is now known as a Whole Systems Thinking approach than when considering business change. Like so many management theories adopted as 'soft strategies' by management consultants, Whole Systems Thinking started in the hard, practical world of manufacturing production planning, where it was developed to help identify and remove bottlenecks on an assembly line.

EM Goldatt first proposed the idea of the Theory of Constraints in his 1984 book *The Goal*.[17] One of the basic tenets he stated was that a system at any one time only has one bottleneck. Applied to production lines or flows of any kind, the principle is that you first need to identify where that bottleneck is and remove it, but that the first rule still applies: the system still has a bottleneck, it's just that now it's somewhere else.

When planning any form of business or organisational change, the same thing is true. Focussing on improving just one part of an overall process may well appear to be successful, but you may simply succeed in moving the problem elsewhere. Unless you consider the effect on the *whole* enterprise, you may actually make things worse.

This is difficult stuff – what team of consultants, keen to present a saleable proposition, and indeed what businesses, needing to look at achievable results, will start with the premise 'we need to look at *everything*'?

It is however telling that in the famous business turnarounds achieved by some of the leaders mentioned in the introduction, such as Jack Welsh or Lou Gerstner, this is precisely what they did. And they did it *before* they came up with their strategy: indeed Lou Gerstner is famous for the reply he gave to the question he was asked about his new vision for IBM just after he'd taken over as CEO in 1993:

'The last thing IBM needs right now is a vision.'[18]

The lesson I took from all this was salutary: when management theories, particularly in the hands of 'management consultants', are brought to bear on a problem, the hardest part is not producing the answer, but properly framing the question and then managing the process. This needs a clear brief, tight control, and the ability to hold said experts effectively to account.

It is telling that in the case of Laura Ashley, none of that was in place, and indeed, the internal team who had designed this brave new world had all (probably wisely) left within six months of it being put into effect.

Lesson 2: If you ever come across an internal customer, show them the door as quickly as possible then change the locks

Joseph Juran has a lot to answer for.[19] In the 1950s he proposed the concept that, as well as the obvious *external* customers which a business has, the individual functions within a business should think of their colleagues in other departments as *internal* customers. Although invented as a way of trying to describe an end-to-end quality control process, his idea has been seized on (and frequently and wilfully misinterpreted) by subsequent generations of so-called change management consultants, usually from the 'why don't we give this a go?' school of strategic planning.

Unfortunately that simple idea, while attempting to create an atmosphere of mutual teamwork and respect for colleagues working on separate parts of a process – and a unified corporate culture – instead gave licence for departments, particularly internal cost functions, to basically forget about the real reason they are there, and for them to focus simply on meeting their own, narrowly defined and often self-set objectives. Taken to its worst excesses, it can encourage cost-side functions to think they should behave as internal suppliers to the 'customers' that they serve. A whole industry springs up which has no place in an efficient organisation: 'client relationship managers'; internal invoicing; and to support it all, an army of accountants. It also carries the risk of creating 'internal competitors', and of other parts of the organisation believing that it is an equally valid option, apparently cheaper even, to look externally for services which are self-evidently available and should be sourced from within. There is a world of difference between the apparent costs of an internal function such as IT or training as presented by a flawed internal recharging mechanism, and the real (in terms of cash) costs of buying the same thing externally.

As Peter Drucker said:

> *'The single most important thing to remember about any enterprise is that results exist only on the outside. The result of a business is a satisfied customer. The result of a hospital is a healed patient. Inside an enterprise there are only costs.* [20]

Two contrasting examples from that time illustrate this perfectly: the first one where Juran's philosophy actually worked as intended, and quality wrinkles were ironed out; but the other engendered completely the opposite behaviour, where, in order to satisfy their own objectives, a function engages in the devious manipulation of information in order to be *appearing* to satisfy their customer's needs.

The average roll length conundrum

At the same time as the new warehouse was being built, a state-of-the-art factory, Texplan, was also being built in Newtown. Matching Laura Ashley's ambition, this was at the time the largest single-span unsupported roof structure in the UK. New machinery was installed, and the facility was officially opened by Diana, Princess of Wales at the beginning of 1987.

As well as paint mixing, it was capable of printing on all types of fabric, which would then be used in LA's garment and home furnishings factories, or shipped to the shops in 35-metre rolls for sale in smaller lengths to customers.

There was only one problem – the rolls weren't actually the right length.

While the company was operating as a single business, this didn't really matter: what was printed was getting sold, and if the stock of fabric metreage wasn't that accurate, well, so be it: the stocks of other things weren't that accurate either.

Once the new structure was put into place, however, it became a critical problem. The Retail division was ordering 35 metres of fabric at a time, but only managing to sell, on average, 32. Whereas Manufacturing were selling profitably, Retail were making a loss on every roll.

Some fairly basic analysis uncovered the problem: virtually none of the rolls received by the Retail division were actually 35 metres – they ranged from 28 metres to 38, with an average of just under 32, a figure matching the actual retail sales.

It turned out that, despite the hi-tech machinery which had been installed in Texplan, one vital piece of equipment had been omitted. Roll batching was being done not by automated measuring systems, but by one man with his foot on a pedal. Following the long Welsh tradition of naming tradesmen after their calling (Organ Morgan, Jones the Milk et al), he was appropriately known as Dai the Batch. The length of the finished roll depended entirely on the level of Dai's concentration, and it transpired, unsurprisingly, that it wasn't up to the task for hours on end.

Once the problem was discovered, it was rapidly fixed with the installation of automated machinery, and standard 35-metre rolls started being produced as advertised.

USA quality 'A'

The early teething problems in Texplan didn't just manifest themselves in roll lengths: the actual quality of the material and printing occasionally left something to be desired too.

Again, in the everyone-working-together ethos which had predominated in the past, this wouldn't have been a huge issue: quality control problems were managed pragmatically so that very few got through to the actual customers, and the business carried on.

With the newly established, and highly expensive, US Retail division, however, this wouldn't do. Shipping even a small percentage of substandard product across the Atlantic was always going to be a problem: stock was in short supply anyway, costs were already too high, and the new US customers were extremely discerning and needing convincing of the quality of this unknown UK retailer. The risk of any less-than-perfect fabric entering the supply chain was therefore unacceptable.

In order to deal with this, rather than push the quality problem right up the supply chain until it was fixed (as had been the case with the roll lengths), a system was devised to perform additional quality checks at the warehouse goods-in dock. All fabric arriving from Texplan, in particular any which could be identified as destined for the USA, was examined with a fine-tooth comb. Normally, on inspection, fabrics had been assigned a 'Quality 1' or 'Quality 2' designation, but now a new 'Quality A' (A for 'America' presumably) was invented, and only the very best was selected and stored in separate warehouse bins ready for picking.

The only problem was that the aforementioned Warehouse Management System, of which both I and Laura Ashley were so proud, wasn't designed to track *three* levels of quality through the physical storage locations, and other than people remembering where they'd put it, there was no other reliable way of picking it. As this change needed to be implemented very quickly in response to loud complaints from across the pond, an ingenious work-around was devised: when the US orders were received and stock was picked, the warehouse staff would attempt to satisfy it from the stock they had separated out, but if there wasn't enough (a common problem as there was no proper merchandise forecasting or production planning yet in place), or the system sent the pickers to somewhere completely different for the stock (which it often did as it wasn't actually aware of its existence), then whatever was actually picked was simply printed as 'Quality A' on the despatch note.

I know, because I was the one who had to code this change, and it took me some while to work out what was going on. The normal process of spelling out the business logic behind a system development was of course going to be impossible without the US catching on, so I was simply instructed to hard-code every roll of fabric destined for the US as 'Quality A'. The despatch targets of the warehouse, along with the personal bonus targets of the management, were thus neatly achieved.

…and not just at Laura Ashley

The last example comes from another company which I did some work for 15 years later – but the story is the same.

Returns processing is very important in running a mail-order business: in the UK the law requires it for distance selling; in fashion retail it is an integral part of the process of choosing and trying on the product; and its smooth operation is a key component of good customer service. It also consumes a huge amount of resources. Laura Ashley had found this out the hard way in the late 1980s, when, as part of its rapid business expansion, it had moved into mail order. There was initially, to all intents and purposes, no functioning returns process, a fact which almost killed the business at birth.

At a catalogue mail-order company in the North West where I did a spell in the early 2000s, as many as 65% of all products were being returned. Before they stuck, some items had been sent out and returned six or seven times. The cost of this in terms of logistics (returns were free to the customer) and reprocessing (often cleaning and always repacking) and write-offs (when product was finally too worn out or damaged to sensibly recycle) was often greater than the gross profit on the item, with inevitable consequences for the bottom line.

Glorified by the important sounding title 'Reverse Logistics', with its own departmental Director, the focus of the organisation was almost entirely on making the process as efficient as possible. Very little was being done, however, to work out why, other than for the reasons stated above, so much merchandise was coming back. It was just accepted that it did.

Ostensibly brought in to look at how to combine the returns functions of two businesses which were in the process of merging, I ended up also running a project to look at *why* as well as *how* returns happened, and the results were revealing.

In the world of mail-order catalogue shopping, there is the inevitable 'rental' market, where clothes as well as other items would be bought and would soon after be returned (confetti in the pockets of the 'didn't quite fit' suit, grass clippings in the 'no longer required' or 'not quite what was wanted' lawnmower), and also a 'not sure what size will fit so I'll order three different ones' business, but this all was accepted as part and parcel of the market in which they were operating. What was less well understood was the degree to which people were buying not clothes, but, as Christian Dior so eloquently (and probably apocryphally) put it regarding perfume, hope. All clothes are arguably aspirational, whether the sharp suit as a projection of business capability and promotion potential, or the nice top in expectation of looking like the model in the catalogue, glamorous or sexy, which, in the case of the returns rate for one particular item of ladies fashion, was exactly the problem.

A chance review of the contact prints[21] from a photo shoot gave us some unexpected clues. The photographer, to get the light levels right or just warm up his subjects before the shoot proper, had been snapping away as the models were getting ready. On the contact paper were shots of the model from behind and well as in front. In order to make look acceptable what everyone in private would have admitted was a very average top, it and the model were pinned, pulled, made up, re-fastened, and ultimately air-brushed to an incredible extent. The resulting catalogue picture showed a beautiful model dressed in the most elegant top, smiling happily at the camera.

The shock for the buyer came when they unwrapped their much-anticipated purchase and put it on. Had it had such a poorly cut sash in the photo? Why did it now fit, not in figure-hugging sexiness, but like the piece of loosely cut sacking it really was? In the case of the sash (a hard-to-believe but absolutely true story), it turned out that the buyer had also disliked it after the photo shoot, and had had it air-brushed out of the final catalogue photo, even though the actual product, of course, had one.

Had it been displayed and photographed accurately, sales may have been much lower (it really was awful), but more of those sales might have stuck. As it was, *more than 90%* of this particular item – which was why we had selected it to study – came back. We marvelled that as many as 100% hadn't.

As a result of this example (and there were many others), a major decision was taken that in the new, merged businesses, there would be *no* Director of Reverse Logistics, and the money saved would be spent on better buying and merchandising. The previous internal focus on excellence of process and internal delivery would be rebalanced by a greater emphasis on the external customer.

Both functions involved in this would have argued (and did) that they were doing an excellent job, and delivering a world-class service to their own internal customers: the marketing department in producing a beautiful catalogue, and the returns department in being as efficient as possible. Both were able to completely ignore the catastrophic impact these individual, but anything but standalone, operations were actually having on both the real customers and the bottom line – a triumph of process over purpose.

Lesson 3: Beware the law of unintended (although, with hindsight, entirely predictable) consequences when designing incentive schemes

The issue which drove the behaviour of the Laura Ashley Distribution division was not in reality very much different from that which seems to have driven Ann Iverson's decision-making during her tenure as CEO. Set very clear objectives, the importance of which would have a significant impact on their personal finances, senior managers focussed solely on the apparent tasks in hand, which in both the above cases were achieved.

As Peter Drucker said:

'What gets measured gets managed; what gets managed gets done.'[22]

But he also said:

'There is nothing quite so useless as doing with great efficiency something that should not be done at all'.[23]

There is much literature about this topic. In the study of economics the hazards presented by inappropriately aligned incentive schemes are often discussed under the heading of Agency Theory.[24] This says that where people have different interests in the same asset, for example CEOs ('Agents') and shareholders ('Principals'), the outcome will always be determined by the way people act, and people always act in their own interests.[25]

The fact that this is now considered a mainstream branch of economics is in itself interesting: Michael J Sandel, in his seminal book *What Money Can't Buy*,[26] argues that whereas economics traditionally has concerned itself with 'inflation and employment, savings and investment, interest rates and foreign trade', it is now more about 'the science of human behaviour'.

This view is developed by Gary Becker:[27] he states that economics is now entirely about that, in that people always 'act to maximise their welfare, whatever activity they are engaged in'. Steven D Levitt goes even further in *Freakonomics*,[28] and simply states that 'incentives are the cornerstone of modern life', and that 'economics is, at root, the study of incentives'. Sandel pinpoints the start of this strand of new economic thought in the 1980s, and especially the influence of the libertarian free-market policies of Thatcher and Reagan. This coincides precisely with the story about Laura Ashley, which, as well as being representative of the ways companies were behaving prior to (and creating the need for) the Cadbury Report, might well have figured as one of his case studies.

Whenever the annual bonus of a departmental head or

a CEO depends on achieving specific targets, be sure that it is highly likely that it will be on those targets, probably to the exclusion of all others, where their focus will be. If they are sufficiently well-aligned with the interests of the other stakeholders involved, then the result will be beneficial, but if they are not, beware.

There are situations, however, where no matter how carefully the targets may be set, or how well intentioned or high-principled the efforts of the participants are to achieve them, because of the design of the system in which they are operating, the only outcome will be failure.

The Beer Game

For several years I taught a module at Cranfield University on System Dynamics (again, nothing to do with IT), as part of which the students, sometimes experienced business people, played a game. The subject has universal appeal, because it concerns a product on which everyone is an expert – beer – and in particular, how to manage the distribution from brewery to consumer.

The Beer Game[29] was invented by a group of professors at the MIT Sloan School of Management in the early 1960s to demonstrate a number of key principles of supply chain systems. It is played by four groups of students who assume the roles of brewer, wholesaler, distributor and retailer. The layout and rules of the game are very simple and fixed: the brewer takes two weeks to brew beer, the wholesaler takes one week to cycle orders and ship them, and the distributor delivers to the end retailer one week after order placement.[30]

The only variable anywhere in the system is customer demand, which is represented by a pile of face-down cards, with a sales figure for the week printed on each one, visible a week at a time only to the retailer.

The purpose of the game is for each player in the supply chain, starting with the retailer, to place orders on *their* supplier for more product based on the information they have. For the retailer, this is the weekly revealed magic number: customer sales. For the others, it is the orders they receive from *their* customers. The way we played it, there were usually two teams of supply chain managers, ostensibly competing with each other, but such competition was irrelevant, as, taking any meaningful measure of success, nobody ever won.

The game was intended to run for 26 weekly cycles, which, even though each cycle only took a few minutes, with the ensuing chaos, shouting and arguments, could take several hours to complete, and the game was often abandoned before the end. The results were always the same: retailers would run out of stock when customer demand was the highest; enormous pools of stock (valued as negative sales) would build in different places, sales would fall through lack of stock, and costs would escalate. There were huge lags in response to orders, and stocks would rise and fall in ever-increasing waves, all of which was completely out of synch with the actual customer demand.

The exercise always ended in much acrimony and mutual finger pointing, and with a huge wash of beer arriving at the retailer far too late, from a brewer who had been totally confused by the increasingly desperate customers further down the supply chain who had been ordering more and more in response to an apparent increase in demand from even lower down, but had not been getting enough stock.

The amazing thing was that none of this was driven by customer behaviour. Unbeknown to the retailer at the outset (and to everyone else for the whole game), customer demand doesn't really change. During the first four weeks, customer demand is identical each week: in week five it steps up a notch (as it can in the real world, maybe in response to some advertising campaign, viral word of mouth or some such stimulus), but then remains unchanged at the new level through the rest of the time. There are no wild fluctuations or erratic buying patterns: after all, average beer consumption is a relatively stable activity.

The system itself defeated even the most experienced supply chain managers: they had no chance. However much they thought they were in control of decision-making (and they were), they were victims of the one thing they could not control; the design of the system itself, which killed them every time.

The lesson of System Dynamics is simple (but very hard to identify and respond to in the real world), and it is that the outputs of a system (whether a supply chain, a remuneration system, the design of an organisation, or in fact any complex set of processes involving human behaviour), are not governed by the inputs, but by the design of the system itself, and the effects of that are impossible to overcome.

Reaching for the stars

An identical, but this time real-world example, concerns the early years of film-related merchandise, specifically *Star Wars* toys. This was possibly the first time the toy industry learnt the very painful lessons which were to frame all its future decision-making, which were that:

- their customers might have been largely adults, but the real drivers of demand were children
- children's attentions and loyalties are very fickle
- parents will do almost anything to acquire something their child desires, and
- all previous methods of assessing customer demand had failed to take into account any of the above.

Over the years, the *Star Wars* film franchise has supported more spin-off merchandise than any other,[31] but in the early days of this new, high-margin revenue stream there was much to learn. Small 3.75" plastic figures of Hans Solo, Darth Vader and R2-D2 could be manufactured for pennies, and sold on the high street for £2. Even including shipping costs, which added a few more pence per item, this was a huge margin. Add to that the fact that they were very collectable, and, initially at least, in short supply, meant that toy retailers could sell as many as they could get their hands on immediately, and without ever having to discount. Perfect!

As the supply chain swung into gear, whole factories, mainly in China and Hong Kong, committed their entire capacity to producing ever more of the little plastic characters. Ships were chartered, more rerouted and reloaded to satisfy the seemingly insatiable market. Times were good, money was being made, and every bit of customer research showed an ever-increasing demand.

For a while in 1990, I did some work for the Tonka Corporation, the latest manifestation of the complex web of toy companies which had merged, demerged and reformed over the years. At that time it was known snappily as Tonka-Kenner-Parker; the Kenner business having recently been acquired on the back of its near collapse.

In 1977, Kenner had acquired the franchise rights to merchandise product branded as *Star Wars*. After a shaky start, sales in the first year reached $100 million worldwide. Kenner continued to introduce waves of action figures from the sequels and in 1984, the year following the release of *The Return of the Jedi*, the range totalled 79 unique character designs. In 1985, the range was renamed Power of the Force and a further 15 figures were released. In total, in addition to board games, vehicles and many other kinds of toys, more than 250 million characters had been sold.

The problem which no-one had thought to consider, however, was how and when all this would stop. And stop it did, almost overnight, with a sudden, complete drying up of sales. The customers, basically fickle, short-attention-span children, had completely stopped buying the beguiling little characters, for any price, and had switched their demands to the newest fashion – *Ghostbusters*.

As students of The Beer Game had been learning the hard way for some years, detecting a change in customer demand anywhere in a supply chain is very hard, and reacting to it in a meaningful way when it's in full flight virtually impossible. Retail demand surveys, for example Nielson in the UK and Verdict in the USA, were still recording huge demand, especially for the harder-to-get toys, but what they failed to do was analyse exactly what that demand was. Desperate parents, trying every avenue to lay their hands on what they believed their beloved offspring wanted, were going from store to store asking the same question. The stores were faithfully recording the apparent demand, and feeding it back to their suppliers and the market research companies. One mother might have asked in half a dozen outlets, plus possibly making several phone calls to stores in nearby towns. Demand was being massively magnified. What the mothers, the stores, the suppliers and the manufacturers were not to know until it was far too late, however, was that, rather than a demand for six million items that month, or even (if they'd bothered to remove the duplicates) one million items, instead the actual *consumer* demand was zero.

Unfortunately for everyone concerned, the factories were still manufacturing products (cost prices having fallen massively due to the huge volumes being churned out), and fleets of ships were still at that moment rounding the Cape of Good Hope packed with containers of toys.

As well as dealing with the financial fallout, which brought several companies to their knees, including Kenner, there remained the problem of what to do with all this unwanted stock. Legend has it that, in the UK, there are disused colliery mineshafts packed with millions of plastic *Star Wars* figures – the sudden demise of coal mining in the mid-1980s conveniently coinciding with the need for vast amounts of immediately available landfill. Ironically, many of these disused mines happened to be in Coalville and the surrounding area, shortly to become the site of the future combined headquarters (once it had been rescued from bankruptcy by its arch rival, Tonka) of Kenner Europe. What future generations of archaeologists, maybe tens of thousands of years hence, will make of this horde of still-perfect, non-biodegradable, plastic figures is unclear: what kind of civilisation might have worshipped such strange icons, and what happened to them? Good questions indeed.

And what happened to Laura Ashley?

With Laura Ashley, it could be argued that it was not the divisionalisation strategy per se or the design of the incentive schemes which created such havoc, but the implementation of the overall system which they represented. And that is certainly something which no-one had spent any time thinking about.

And the result of all this? 25 years of steady growth was brought to a grinding halt. It could be argued that this has still not been recovered 25 years later, although a rights issue in 2003, and aggressive cost-cutting and effective stock control since, seemed to have stabilised the outflows for a while.

In 2004, Laura Ashley exited its Welsh spiritual home in Carno, and a few years later closed the warehouse in Newtown. Texplan has been sold to the management, and is now trying to make its way as an independent printing and paint factory. The European business, much as in the US, was sold to its management, this time for 3 euros.

Today the company is worth £112 million, and with the payment of a first dividend in 2013 and subsequent bi-annual payments, majority owner MUI is finally getting a little of its money back. There is cash as well as freehold property on the balance sheet (although largely offset by its final salary pension fund deficit), and, thanks to hard work by Lillian Tan who stepped down as CEO in 2011, sales and margins have been slowly improving, at least in the UK.

While it could be argued that Laura Ashley was a child of its time, and should have faded away many years ago, it is still hanging on. It is just as arguable, however, that, through a combination of mismanagement and poor leadership, it was probably dealt what will eventually prove to be its death blow in the late 1980s, and is merely taking its time to die.

GONE FOR A BURTON

1

In 1991 The Burton Group was on exactly the opposite swing of the pendulum to Laura Ashley – the company had been essentially a collection of separate warring factions for some time, each trading division run as a mini fiefdom under the watchful overall eye of Ralph Halpern, who encouraged the fighting much as a Roman emperor might have egged on the gladiators.

Unfortunately for this management style, the heady pile-'em-high, sell-'em-cheap days of the 1980s were over. Halpern himself, to the press the epitome of corporate and personal excess, had left with a £2 million pay-off and an annual pension of £456,000, and a new broom in the form of the abrasive American John Hoerner was about to take over and clean out the Augean stables.

Although Halpern was out, it arguably wasn't lack of retail success which finished him off. The Burton Group, after all, was the 'university of retail', the training ground over the years for anyone who was anyone in British fashion retailing, including Terry Green, Angus Monro, Stuart Rose, John Coleman, and many more.[32] It was rather a combination of some financially disastrous property deals made during the 'race for space', and a rebellion against what shareholders were now seeing as the excesses of corporate greed.

At its peak in 1991, the group had around 1,700 stores[33] and employed more than 60,000 people. The growing Topshop and the still profitable Dorothy Perkins were driving sales. As well as the small-space 'multiples' businesses, Halpern had acquired the large-space department store retailers Debenhams and Harvey Nichols, which he saw as his crowning achievements.

I joined in 1991 as IT Director for the 'multiples' side of the business, the 1600 'small space' (as distinct from the department) stores; part of the centralised group IT function, MBS – Multiples Businesses' Systems, (but without the apostrophe).

Once again it was an exciting time to be working in IT. Behind every distinct brand was an equally distinct army of people replicating back-office functions: from buying, where often six different buyers were sitting down with suppliers such as Levi's, who were laughing all the way to the bank; to retail operations (where different area managers would visit different stores which were next door to each other); and systems. This was particularly true in merchandise planning, where, because of lack of scale and the divisions' continued preference (despite or, more probably, because of MBS) for small, often feral, internal IT departments, much was manual and spreadsheet-based.

Some consolidation had taken place, but half-heartedly: in the stores, multiple Electronic Point of Sale (EPoS) till systems had been reduced to just two solutions; in head office, multiple transactional Buying and Merchandising systems to a mere four. The largest two divisions by turnover, Burton Menswear and Dorothy Perkins, had pooled resources for mutual self-protection as much as anything as the headwinds of a changed high-street economy had started to blow, but the smaller, emerging brands such as Topshop and Principles were aggressively ploughing their own furrows.

In the back office, all the signs of organisational dysfunction were there: internal customers; duplicated, overlapping functions doing the same things differently; and armies of accountants, a sure sign of an organisation which has lost control – even my newly inherited IT department had three to manage the internal recharging.[34]

Hoerner, however, preached a new mantra – standardisation and automation, all to be done with a ruthless eye on the bottom line.

And so the snappily-named IFPR project was born.

Merchandise planning is a huge, data intensive activity, and before we go any further, I need to warn you to hang on to your hats. To quote Slartibartfast in *The Hitchhiker's Guide to the Galaxy:* 'This next bit may disturb you. It scares the willies out of me.' Depending on decisions about breadth and depth, in fashion, a season of 26 weeks might involve planning several thousand lines by week, in both units and value, with maybe ten attributes to be input or calculated for each. Attributes such as unit cost, sale price, markdown budget, inventory, balance to achieve, open to buy, cover, stock-to-sales ratio and numerous measures of margin at different levels; and that is even before the complexities of size ratios and store distribution come into play.[35] It is the complex product of a top-down financial budget, plus bottom-up, product-sales-driven process, involving numerous iterations until the projected income from the sum total of all the products which are actually going to be ordered (and hopefully sold) matches the overall departmental, and ultimately company, budget plan. It is broken down into season, month and week, as well as into department, sub-department and product category. One season's plan, once sizes and stores are factored in, can total more than 1,000,000,000 (one BILLION!) data items.[36]

For all this, you need a system, and a mighty powerful one.

What The Burton Group had instead was an enormous army of people equipped with spreadsheets. Hoerner recognised a huge opportunity here, not only for cost-saving through automation, but also for far better decision-making through speed and especially accuracy, for while the spreadsheets and reports appeared on cursory inspection to produce coherent plans, in reality, with the numerous iterations, copies, consolidations, manual alterations and reworks, it was impossible to know what they truly represented.[37]

After a short period of great secrecy and not a lot of preparation, a team was assembled and the project was launched one Friday in February 1992, when 933 people were made redundant and left the building the same day.[38] The plan was to replace the work they did with a new system, running on one central database, totally integrated and fully automated, and it would be delivered by the end of August that same year – six months hence.

IT people often rail against 'artificial deadlines', but there was nothing artificial about this one: September was the start of full-on planning (already a very late date) for the Spring/Summer '93 season's stock, and until then, all merchandise planning activity was effectively suspended and the company was in freefall.

What's in a name?

All systems end up with a name. Really important developments by large technology companies will often start off having a 'working title' ('Silverlake', 'Threshold' or some such), and the final name will be dreamt up by marketing people before the system sees the light of day (usually something far less interesting, like 'OS/400' or 'Windows 10', the final customer names for those much more thrillingly-named IBM and Microsoft projects). Internal software developments, on the other hand, usually end up with techie acronyms invented by programmers who tend to think in abbreviations. With the new Integrated Forecasting and Performance Reporting system, there was no time to spend on such frivolities, so after a very brief but ultimately fruitless session one evening in a local pub, the project simply went on calling itself by its wordy description, Integrated Forecasting and Performance Reporting, shortened to its initials: IFPR. It stuck, and for years afterwards everyone simply referred to it as If/Pr, pronounced with two equally ungainly syllables.

And so the project started. My role as IT Director was to ensure the system got delivered, so the best people were assembled – mainly ones I'd worked with before and who had joined me at Burtons: people whom I knew would be able to cut the code as well as the mustard, and not need too much management to get it done on time.

One of the biggest issues we had to deal with was team communications. The retail business was run out of central London, with the various chains and corporate offices of The Burton Group occupying most of the prestigious buildings (which at that time they still owned) on the north side of Oxford Street running east from Oxford Circus. For historical reasons, the MBS development team was based in Leeds, on the Hudson Road site of the original manufacturing facility, Progress Mills, built in 1909 (along with houses, shops, canteens, medical facilities and sports fields) for what grew to be a workforce of 10,000 staff. Bespoke tailoring, on which Montague Burton's reputation had been built, was long gone – replaced by overseas-manufactured, off-the-peg suits – and the site was now the base of the 'offshored' (i.e. not occupying expensive London real estate) support services, including IT, accounts and warehousing.[39]

I had to be in both locations: because of the poor esteem in which MBS had been held, and the previous plan I had inherited on joining (which was to close the Leeds part of the department down), it was deemed unacceptable for me, as IT Director and part of the management team, to be based anywhere other than in London. As all of my department were actually in Leeds, this made commuting a pretty much full-time occupation. During the spring and summer of that year I drove just under 1000 miles per week, which was actually a distance greater than I had covered commuting each week from mid-Wales to southern Holland whilst doing the Laura Ashley project, including the sea journey. It had its benefits though: instead of access to continental-priced Amstel, in the nights I used to stay over in Leeds, I was guaranteed a plentiful supply of a far more (for a Northerner) palatable tipple, Tetley's bitter.

Fortunately for me, this period coincided with the availability of early mobile car phones; unfortunately for other members of the team, who remember it with anything but fondness, it was an analogue service, and the signal along much of the M1 was notoriously bad.

Naming of parts

One of the most important (and surprising) things IFPR had to address was how the business actually measured things. These were important things too, things such as sales, stock and profit. It might seem amazing that these were not already in place, and in a sense they were, but it quickly emerged that every chain, and indeed every department (represented by every spreadsheet), had a slightly, or in some cases very different, definition of, for example, what 'margin' was.

IFPR was tasked with gaining agreement on what these basic definitions should be; after all, if a dumb computer is going to calculate something, it can only do so if it's told what the exact formula is.

In Financial Accounting, measures have long been precisely defined, although are still open to creative accounting in their representation.[40] In Management Accounting and particularly merchandise performance reporting, no such rules apply; and when ownership of the company's key performance measures, and responsibility for their definition, rests not with the Finance department, which is the centre of control in most businesses, but with the Buying and Merchandising (B&M) function, then it is reasonable to assume that what is produced may not have quite the same rigour.

It would surely be a simple job to propose a common set of definitions and implement them? Unfortunately not, as it turned out.

Take just one example from the dozens which needed to be agreed: NAMAD (Net Achieved Margin after Discount), a measure accepted, even then, as a good indication of the real profitability of a product. But that apparently even well stated term proved one of the hardest. Of the five words in the title, two of them contain lots of wriggle room. 'Net'? Net of what? It turned out that the chains couldn't agree even whether that included VAT or not. And as for discount, that word alone was the subject of many hours of anguished wrangling. Did it include markdown? (It was agreed that it didn't: that would become a whole new opportunity for disagreement.) Vouchers? 2-4-1s (known then and ever since by the elegant phrase invented in the 1980s by Topshop – BOGOF, Buy One Get One Free)? Manager's specials (damaged stock, 'mates' rates', and the like)? And what about returns, shouldn't they be taken into account before real profitability was determined, and if so, how?

The process also opened up old wounds in the perennial battle between the B&M department and Finance. The Finance department saw this as an opportunity to gain control; after all, they knew all about setting common definitions and doing sums (didn't they?), and therefore it was they who should be trusted with coming up with the definitions. Unfortunately for them, in fashion retail no-one takes much notice of Finance. Unlike in some other businesses, (even other types of retail businesses such as one we will look at in a later chapter, electricals, where the real money is made through rigorous cost control and selling things such as accessories and extended warranties), in fashion, the *vast bulk* of the money is made on the margin. Gross margins (i.e. the simple difference between what a product costs and what it can be sold for) can be as high as 95%: the trick is to sell as much of the stock at full price as quickly as possible. The most powerful tool a fashion retailer has at their disposal is the ability to discount, or 'mark down', the product as the season progresses or opportunity rises (Blue Cross days, pre-Christmas sales and the like), and the markdown budget is the biggest line in any departmental plan; bigger often than the cost of buying the products in the first place. The most grievous crime a merchandiser can commit is not the one of having leftover stock at the end of the season (a bad enough misdemeanour in itself); it's not having completely spent the markdown budget to shift it. None of this is under the control of the Finance department, who are left to count the crumbs and make up (sometimes literally) the numbers.

When the new definitions were in danger of exposing the fact that that oh-so-lovely light blue top of last season hadn't actually made any money at all, the buyers would then immediately retreat into the fluffy world of fashion marketeers everywhere, and try to fudge the whole issue of scientific measurement by saying that without that top, then they wouldn't have sold any of the matching dark blue skirts, and that was where the money was. A niggling doubt remained, of course, that the reason why the buyer was being so defensive wasn't because of some subtleties of product mix, but that they'd overcommitted to a huge delivery of them.

Hoerner, however, was having none of this. He had already said he would act as ultimate arbiter on any major disagreements which we couldn't resolve ourselves; someone only had to bring the issue to him personally and he would make a decision. The process became instantly much simpler when the first of the most outspoken heads of department went to him to say she didn't agree with what was being proposed, and he immediately fired her. To my recollection, every other proposal was agreed without dissent.

The issue of having to define apparently obvious and supposedly already well-understood terms – ones which have often been in general use for many years in the business – is a surprisingly common activity within many systems projects. Companies, often for the first time, have to face up to the fact that, up until then, they didn't actually know how they were doing. Usually it is not important what the precise definitions are, only that they are identical everywhere so that proper like-for-like comparisons can be made: Is this product doing better than that one? Is that store doing better? Is this season better than last?

It is an especially difficult challenge when those systems are going to span divisions, companies, or even countries. It may be that the project discovers that the issues are unsurmountable, and as we shall see when we look at Compass Group later, lead to new thinking about how to organise and manage a large, distributed organisation.

It would be reasonable to think this might be an old problem, addressed long ago in all companies; but when I was at Dixons – as recently as 2008 – as part of implementing a new system, we ran a project to do exactly the same thing, ironically for the financial accounts.

Thanks to the team…

The project team who were engaged in developing IFPR totalled less than ten people: three in London who had expertise in both merchandise planning and business analysis and design, and a small development team in Leeds whose job it was to create the numerous code iterations which would ultimately (and hopefully) become the new system.

They all worked incredibly long hours over that summer, giving up weekends as well as holidays for the duration, and without this the project would not have been a success.

To cut a not very long but very intense story short, the system was delivered in the required six months, the work of 933 people was replaced by one computer system, and the Spring/Summer 1993 collection was successfully planned, launched and subsequently managed.

What happened in subsequent years, however, was a different story.

2

The question is, did this ambitious project work?

In the sense that it delivered exactly what it set out to do (rare in systems-driven business change projects), it achieved its goals, and I believe that without it, Hoerner's strategy would not have got off the ground. Carl McPhail, later CEO of New Look, but who at the time worked for Hoerner, remembers the systems and processes that were put in place. '*They were well ahead of their time. It became a benchmark*', he says.[32]

The back-office consolidation, though, was only part of the plan. At the same time as the company was implementing the new systems, it was also reviewing two other key areas: retail space and the supply chain. Of the 1600+ small space stores, many were, because of the changing nature of the high street, clearly now in the wrong place; and of those which did occupy good locations, many required rebranding as they were the wrong size or too close to others in the same chain for the new shopping patterns which were emerging. In 1993, project 'Townprint' was launched to address this, as a result of which 380 units were disposed of, 228 new ones were acquired, and 354 units were rebranded from one chain to another. This required a monumental effort, and to tackle it, a centralised stores team (including IT) was created to manage disposals, acquisitions and refits.

The supplier base was tackled with project 'Fastflow'. Part of this was targeted at reducing the huge number of merchandise suppliers, from more than 1400 to just under 700. The major part, however, was building on the new management information coming out of IFPR to speed up the supply chain. In the past, in order to ensure good supply, standard practice as well as practical necessity had meant having to commit to large one-off purchases of stock long before the season got underway. This manufacturing-led approach was always high-risk, with little flexibility to react to the customer demand after the initial launch, and consuming a large amount of cash tied up in stock in the external supply chain or Burton's own warehouses. Fastflow focussed on using only the most responsive of suppliers (which was the main factor in the huge reduction), but also moving stock quickly through distribution points rather than simply storing it ('cross-docking'[41]), and having a much more responsive replenishment cycle based on real-time information from the new systems.

These were all laudable programmes, but whether it was a deliberate strategy, or simply the consequence of the intense focus on the back office, as buying processes were combined, retail merchandising was centralised, and brand marketing resources were pooled, the ruthless standardisation and homogenisation also started leaking through to the front of house, to the customer-facing aspects of the chains themselves.

On the high street and in the shiny new shopping centres, joint-sites were combined wherever possible: Dorothy Perkins and Burton Menswear started sharing similar adjoining facia, stock rooms and even staff; and to save on brand development costs for the department stores, and provide additional selling space at a marginal cost for the small-space retailers, shop-in-shops became the norm. Principles, Dorothy Perkins and Burton Menswear started appearing as 'brands' in Debenhams.

At the same time, Hoerner went on a buying spree: the small-space retailers might have been struggling for their own identities, and the customer might have been losing track of who these previously distinctive brands now were, but this did not stop him from increasing both the number of brands and the number of outlets (to more than 2000), with the purchase of Sears Womenswear (and with it the Miss Selfridge and Wallis brands) and Wade-Smith.

By 1995 The Burton Group seemed to be on the road to recovery, posting albeit modest after-tax profits of £73 million on a turnover of £2 billion.

The sheer size of this empire, however, now meant that the company was starting to run into *dis-economies* of scale, especially as the far fewer large-space department stores required very different disciplines to run them well and the complexity generated by the shop-in-shop approach wasn't serving either of them very well.[42] Customers too were drifting away and sales were falling at even the old stalwarts.

Eventually, in January 1998, Debenhams was spun off, partly because it didn't fit in, and partly because the management of such a monster small-space multiples empire (now to be known as Arcadia – the 'new world') required dedicated focus.[43]

John Hoerner was finally replaced in 2000 as Arcadia's CEO by the old Halpern protégé, Stuart Rose, who had lost his job when Debenhams was sold in favour of his old rival Terry Green.

3

So what lessons did I learn from all of this?

Lesson 1: Business benefits aren't business benefits until they're in the bank

The unfortunate reality is that most IT-driven business change projects fail. The reason usually given is that one or more of the three traditional measures of project success, Time, Budget and Function, was deemed to have been missed. Whether that is because the measures were defined, maybe prematurely, a little too tightly, or whether the project team simply failed to deliver effectively will always be a point of debate. Despite the focus on them however, at the end of the day these are not the real reason projects fail; the real reason is because they don't actually deliver what was promised, which is the business benefits.

For me, as well as the excitement of delivering such a

critical and high-profile system from scratch, IFPR was a powerful lesson (human cost aside) in business benefit delivery: be ruthless, take the benefits as much as possible upfront, then use the system to leverage change.

Evaluating and then delivering business benefits is a hotly debated topic when deciding whether to introduce new IT systems. It is often pointed out (but less often practised) that identification of the former should precede and drive the decision to do the latter; however, in many situations, it is surprisingly often the other way round.

Two fundamentally different reasons are given for making changes: necessity and opportunity. And, as they imply very different start points for the business cases, we shall examine both.

The burning platform

The starkest necessity is that of the 'burning platform',[44] which can appear to offer a get-out-of-jail-free card to proposers of business cases. However hard to swallow, the argument put simply goes: 'unless we do this, we are dead'. What proponents of this school of persuasion often choose to gloss over, however, is a full explanation of the dilemma facing someone standing on a burning platform, whose only options are to stay put or jump into the void below. The choice is not between certain death or a healthy future; it is between certain death and merely probable death. Making the jump is not offering a guarantee of success, but rather the prospect (and possibly a very distant one) of something potentially only marginally better.

The year 2000 problem was an excellent and possibly unique example of this kind of 'burning platform' business case. No-one really knew what was going to happen, least of all the software experts. In this case, it is likely that everyone involved, including business as well as IT managers, secretly welcomed an excuse to replace fragile or out-of-date systems without having to go through all the pain and pretence of business-benefit justification. Here it was simple: unless we bite the bullet, we may not have a business to run come 01/01/2000.

To the great joy of software suppliers and management consultancies, almost every business which had been around for a while was engaged in this in the years leading up to 2000, backed up in this case by shareholders who were demanding the reassurance of a well-founded Y2K programme as a sign of good corporate governance. Many systems got replaced or upgraded, and actually much good was probably done in shaking off the dust of the past. No hard number business cases however were ever produced for any of this – boards understandably shied away from pricing the upside as the value of the entire company, and instead attributed it to 'maintenance'. A few took the opportunity to have a more thorough cleanout and were able to treat the cost as an exceptional item without it having a material effect on either the operating profit or share price of the business.[45]

Such burning platform justifications however, as well as being very rare, are also very hard to get away with, in that business leaders are often (rightly) sceptical of proponents of the 'we have no other choice' school of persuasion: after all, there are always choices, even if the alternative, which as a minimum is to do nothing, could be fatal.

Most projects, therefore, need to find a solid, financially robust justification for embarking on them. This is especially true of major business change projects, where, as well as the hard costs and, hopefully, hard benefits, there will undoubtedly also be complex and difficult-to-deal-with 'soft' costs (lost opportunity, organisational distraction, people issues and the like) to absorb.

Such projects then must identify the opportunities as well as the costs, and express them in terms which make sense. And so business benefit cases are born.

Business benefit cases self-evidently have two equally important, dimensions: on the one hand, costs, and on the other, benefits, and both need to be properly researched, quantified and strongly challenged. Only when all the costs (when properly taken into account and appropriately adjusted upwards) are far enough surpassed by the benefits (when properly identified and appropriately adjusted downwards) is the project worth doing. And even then, it is only worth doing if there is not some other competing project on the table which would deliver an even bigger return for the same deployment of resources. In other words, doing one project has a hidden cost, which is the cost of not doing an alternative one. This is called 'opportunity cost', and we will come across this again later.

There are many costs in systems change projects, some of which are not identified at all. Put simply, costs can be represented as upfront implementation costs (such as new software, new or upgraded hardware, people time – both internal as well as external – plus risk management contingencies), and in addition, the ongoing costs of owning the solution longer term (including day-to-day support, upgrades, maintenance fees, network rentals and the like, as well as the profit impact of capital depreciation). Ongoing maintenance is the elephant in the room in many IT departments.

Maintenance v. investment

The initial cost of replacing a system should not to be confused with that other hard to understand (if you're a CFO or CEO) cost of IT – maintenance. What appear to be huge, impenetrable and surprising large ongoing costs always seem to come with any IT system. Despite this being the case, they usually get ignored in the original reckoning, either because of the inexperience or lack of foresight of the people involved (whether managers in IT or other parts of the business), or because it is inconvenient or even fatal to the business case. IT maintenance costs include such necessities as repairing the software or hardware when it fails (as it periodically will), keeping it up to date with the latest releases (sometimes a functional benefit or security necessity; sometimes merely a supplier wheeze to justify generating further fees), or simply supporting it in an environment of insufficiently expert or new users.

It is an unfortunate but undeniable fact that as well as

hardware getting old, tired and eventually failing, so does software. This statement should not be as surprising as it sounds: constant tinkering (in the form of urgent, so maybe suboptimally applied, bug fixes); new functionality, in the name of responsiveness, hastily bolted on; and changes to the environment in which it operates all contribute to gradual software fatigue. Eventually, the system can become so unreliable, complex and therefore risky, or just impossible to support, that the only option is to replace it. This way forward, however, particularly in organisations which have lived with and contributed to the worsening of the situation for some time, and where the sheer complexity of the resulting infrastructure is deeply embedded, is fraught with difficulty.

In extreme cases, the high cost of maintenance and support can consume nearly all the budget of an IT department. Business leaders (especially CFOs) look at the cost of IT and rebel instinctively at what they see as extortionate costs which appear to deliver no real value to the business. And while that is partly true, these costs are not there to deliver 'new value' (the misconception that an IT department's entire function is to develop new things), but are there as a result of previous projects which have gone live, maybe some time ago; the sum total of every bit of software, hardware, network and support need from all the past projects. This maintenance of what has become known as the 'legacy infrastructure' is what most IT departments spend most of their time, and almost all of their money, managing. The most important job is not to add new value; it's to prevent new costs through operational failure.

For this reason, many organisations end up with increasingly burdensome cost-bases for their systems, and increasingly fragmented operations. Banks, for example, which have often inherited systems from acquisitions of other institutions, including products which may have lifespans in excess of 25 years, can be stuck with multiple, highly expensive legacy systems. In the inherently high-cost world of finance, however, these are seen simply as the cost of doing business.[46]

The most forward-looking businesses work very hard to avoid this issue, and we will look at one such business, easyJet, in a later chapter; but as we shall see when we look at another, Dixons Stores Group (DSGi when I joined), this problem can become so intractable that it becomes a major threat to business growth.

As well as the ongoing costs of a new system, what is often missed is also the cost of actually delivering the benefits; the assumption being that because they have been identified, and the solution has been implemented, they will deliver themselves without further effort. IFPR was the exception which proves the rule: in other projects, as a minimum there will be new and continued training to deliver as people adapt to the new processes (critical to prevent them reverting to the old ones, sometimes with the resulting complete disuse of the new system). There should also be people tasked with explicitly tracking the delivery of the benefits, and this too costs money.

All these costs add up to what is known in the trade as the Total Cost of Ownership (TCO), and across the five years that may be considered as a sensible time over which to evaluate benefits and therefore payback, they can be as great, or greater, than the original project costs. To ignore them would therefore seem to be somewhat foolish.[47]

On the other side of the equation, benefits come in two flavours: these are commonly referred to as 'hard' (bankable, built into business plans, profit-affecting), and 'soft' (more than just nice-to-haves and *hopefully* profit-affecting, but nevertheless difficult to measure directly in simple monetary terms). These latter ones often include such prophesies as 'a more motivated or agile workforce', 'better information' (the implication that this leads to better decision-making) or 'faster speed to market'. Certainly these things have value, but by business benefits, what *should* be meant are only the hard numbers: things that can be identified, measured and actually done in order to improve the financial performance of a business. A good test is whether corollaries or proxies can be identified for the soft benefits: for example 'a more motivated workforce' might be measured in terms of lower staff turnover; 'faster speed to market' as a lower stock holding, both of which are measurable numbers and have hard financial values.

The key thing is that to be real, *all* benefits must have clear owners who identify with and support them from the outset, and can then be held accountable for their delivery. If the benefits are to be found in 'better purchasing' for example (a topic covered in more detail in the Compass Group case study later), then whoever is responsible for them should have them built into their budgets upfront: if the new system is forecast to save £10 million per year, then the cost of purchasing next year should be planned to be

£10 million less. Taking a lesson about organisational design and using properly structured incentives schemes to create the right outcomes from the Laura Ashley story, the Head of Purchasing's bonus must be on the line.

Very often, however, such benefits are hypothetical (existing only in the imagination of the proposer and the cells of a spreadsheet) or worse, illusory. In the example above, that £10 million might well have been calculated simply as a 1% saving on a £1 billion total purchasing budget.

This presents two opposing difficulties: on the one hand, 1% of any large number is very attractive on a simplistic level, and if the costs of raw materials purchased are 50% of the price of the goods sold, as they can be in foodservice, what self-respecting CFO wouldn't want to add that 0.5% margin to the bottom line? The other difficulty though is that 1% is a statistically insignificant fraction, hard to measure or prove, and very hard to separate from other, maybe greater, variables that will probably change over the same period: raw materials alter in price; volumes go up as businesses expand thus generating greater discounts; and, equally common but fatal for ensuring the projected return is delivered, new people are now in place who no longer subscribe to those targets. Typically, payback periods are calculated over five years, which is a very long time in most businesses: once the new system is in place, people, often worn out by the pain and difficulty of implementation, simply want to move on.

What was so astonishing therefore about the hard benefits of IFPR was that they were taken immediately, before the IT system was in place. The benefit case was straightforward, so it was banked.

This goes completely against the traditional hockey-stick-shaped benefits curve which is the reality (if rarely acknowledged at the time) for most systems projects: i.e. 'we'll spend all or most of the money upfront, and then, after the disruptive impact on the business and further opportunity costs of going live have been absorbed, we'll hopefully start getting something back'. This hockey stick stretches into a (by definition) different future, one where often so much has changed in the underlying assumptions, or so much has been learnt about where the real benefits may otherwise lie, that the return on the original investment is never achieved or even tracked.

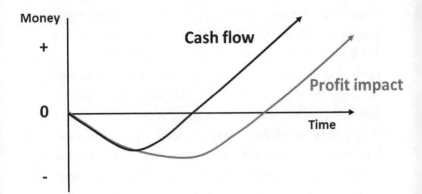

Cash and benefits curve of a typical IT project

Very few businesses create genuine business benefit delivery plans – they simply identify the (usually *potential*) benefits and fail to define by whom, with what or exactly how they need to be delivered, or to track after the event whether they have been.

With IFPR, the benefits usually defined as 'soft' (i.e. in most projects, unlikely ever to be delivered in a measurable financial sense), in this case became the real focus after implementation and were also delivered through the new system within the next 12 months. These included the huge upside of being able to create the new seasons' plans in just a few short weeks rather than months and with the certain knowledge that they were sound, at least in the sense that they actually added up.

Rewards for early EPoS adopters

Benefits are not always to be found where they are expected. As late as 1991, when I first joined The Burton Group, it was still manually recording some sales. A workforce of several hundred (in the past it had been several thousand) staff – all women – were every weekend punching Kimball tags. This early precursor to the barcode contained enough information in the form of punched holes for it to be read by a machine but required the tags to be couriered back to head office where the highly expensive equipment was situated. In the not-very-distant past, 100% of sales had been recorded in this way.[48] Kimball tags had been developed originally by Sears, Roebuck and Company in the USA in 1952 and their use had spread across North American and European retailers. Whilst providing a degree of accuracy in tracking stock and sales, it was always a 'batch process' in that the tags were batched up together and only entered into the system some time after the sales had taken place, on a weekly cycle. While it meant the stock and sales information was then up to date, it was too long after the event, and lagging far too much behind what was really happening, to provide any useful information. It supported reporting, but not action. We have already seen, in the simulated example of The Beer Game and the real world one of the Star Wars toys in the preceding chapter, how a lag in information can create havoc in the decision-making process.

The very first adopters of EPoS systems in stores were persuaded to deploy it (again, it was a very expensive solution) as a way of automating and speeding up this sales recording. They expected to get a return, albeit a small one, from not having to rent the Kimball punching and reading machines and from labour savings, and indeed this was the case.

What they hadn't predicted was the huge upside from getting real-time information on stock and sales. What made this possible were two things: the replacement of the cumbersome, batch-processed Kimball tags with the newly developed barcode and its associated standard coding agreements; and the ability to communicate electronically with the tills in the stores via dial-up modems once the shop had closed for the day and then to process this data into the stock and sales systems that night. This sudden access to almost real-time information allowed much more accurate store replenishment to take place, replacing items sold the previous day almost immediately and allowing decisions to be taken on reordering or discontinuing lines depending on how they were performing on a daily basis.

This new flexibility and responsiveness had the effect of shortening supply chains and releasing much-needed locked-up cash. In the grocery business, PWC estimated in 1999 that the total benefit to producers, distributors, retailers and consumers of having a standardised, low-cost, machine-readable barcode on every product in the US came to $17 billion annually.[49]

While all this seems perfectly normal nowadays (with real-time sales tracking and when the time from new product design to availability in the shop can be as short as two weeks), in the 1970s it was revolutionary.

How to ensure benefits actually get delivered

My namesake, John Thorp, describes in his book *The Information Paradox*[50] the three conditions necessary for successful business benefit delivery, namely i) what he calls Activist Accountability, ii) Relevant Measurement, and iii) Proactive Management of Change.

Activist Accountability is the first, and he doesn't mean just pre-allocated accountability for business benefit delivery as discussed above. Here, he means *everyone* who has a specific job to do. He cautions though against simply saying things like 'everyone is accountable for the success of this project': as he points out, 'if everyone is accountable for everything, then in real terms, nobody is accountable for anything'.[ibid]

On IFPR, accountabilities for delivery at every stage

were crystal clear, and minds were focussed by making sure future bonus opportunities were closely linked to results.

Project bonuses are a contentious topic: on the one hand they can be highly effective (because, as we've seen before, incentive schemes play into that human factors sphere of economics which says ultimately everyone acts in their own self-interest), but on the other hand, particularly for a company which is not making any money and therefore not paying bonuses to anyone else, they can be seen as divisive and unfair. They can also be criticised for employing a 'jumping for jelly-beans'[51] approach to team motivation, in that surely this is what people are employed to do, and how much more do you have to offer them next time to do the same thing?

For a project team, however, deliberately set up away from the everyday business and given a specific, highly mission-critical task, it can be an effective tool. And there wasn't going to be a next time: this was make or break.

The other two necessary conditions (Relevant Measurement and Proactive Management of Change) were already in place: measurement of benefits involved counting the money already in the bank (about £25 million in cost savings), and the change required to achieve them had already taken place.

Resistance is futile

Implementing the required changes successfully is at the core of benefit delivery. Professor Denis Protti, in discussing the challenges in the UK healthcare sector, sums this up in a neat mathematical equation:

$$f(D, V, S) > R$$

In other words, if any meaningful progress is to be made, a combination of Dissatisfaction with the present situation (D), the existence of a Vision of a more desirable future (V), and the knowledge of the first Steps to take in moving towards that future (S) must be greater than the Resistance to change (R).

As he says, 'if any of the first three factors are missing, then change will not take place successfully, no matter how strong the other factors'.[52]

IFPR satisfied all of these: the present situation was that the merchandising planning function and current systems had already been dispensed with (an act of bravado as impressive as and not dissimilar to that of the Spanish Conquistador Hernán Cortés, who, landing on the shores of Mexico with 600 men in 1519, was so confident of his certain success that he quite literally burnt his bridges, or more specifically in this case, his boats); it was crystal clear what needed to be done; and it was also clear there was only one way to go. The other side of the equation was also aided enormously by there being no-one left in the building who was going to offer any resistance anyway.

The history of the evolution of Information Technology is often described as having three phases: firstly Automation (replacing manual labour with computers), Information (using electronic data as a source of management reporting) and lastly Business Transformation (using systems to fundamentally change the underlying processes and therefore the way an organisation works).[53]

As if the ambition wasn't already great enough, IFPR also tackled all three aspects in one go. It was going to automate what were previously manual spreadsheet systems; provide performance reporting and real-time feedback loops where hitherto little had existed; and it was going to change completely the organisation and processes, as well as the timescales for merchandise planning.

On the positive side, as well as strong project leadership (as opposed to management – see later), it had in the form of John Hoerner an 'Impatient Visionary', identified by Joyce, Nohria and Roberson in *What Really Works: The 4+2 Formula for Sustained Business Success* as one of the key drivers of project success.[54] This role they consider vital for rapid delivery; because this person is single-mindedly focussed on what they want to achieve, they can overcome what is often the biggest hidden obstacle, namely the 'belief that compromise is needed to succeed'.

John Hoerner was under no such illusions, and the project team were empowered to make their own decisions knowing that they would be fully supported.

Lesson 2: Not all artificial deadlines are actually artificial

As discussed by Fred Brooks[55] in the seminal *Mythical Man-Month*, while it may not be possible to replace one woman taking nine months to have a baby with nine women taking one, the allegedly unalterable laws of project physics can actually be significantly bent. By using many of the other ideas in the book (the surgical team, conceptual integrity, specialised tools, of which more later), IFPR was delivered by the very real deadline, the start of planning for the next season. Setting aggressive, seemingly impossible, targets proved that truly extraordinary things can be achieved in very little time if everyone is properly equipped to do it and motivated enough, but it is true that this goes against the grain for most projects, and it requires a completely different approach to project planning.

It is a truth universally acknowledged (or at least rigorously taught in project management masterclasses) that in all projects there are three interconnected and supposedly immutable variables: Time, Resources and Output. Time and resources are of course both costs and together make up (at least in theory) total effort, so they can be used in a nicely balanced mathematical equation:

$$Resources \times Time = Effort\ In = Output\ produced$$

Traditionalists will therefore have it that if a greater output is required, then it can only be achieved by increasing time or resources. Alternatively, given a certain amount of time and resources, only so much can be done. Output is usually expressed as Scope in project terms; an increase in scope automatically triggering a call for more money, resources and/or time in the traditional project manager's mind.

While this second statement is generally applicable, it does not follow that the first one is too. It was amazing on

IFPR how much more could be squeezed into the same pint pot as and when it was identified. And it had to be: the business had to have the basic minimum in place to enable it to start the planning process on time. This was not about eliminating 'nice to haves' (they were already long gone), this was about ensuring that once planning started, it would be robust.

The concept of 'baselining' a project plan is deeply engrained in traditional project management thinking: i.e. once the three variables of scope, resources and time are 'agreed', then the movement of any one of them constitutes a change to this baseline, and can only be accomplished via a 'change-request' which creates a new baseline.

This discipline of Project Change Management (as distinct from that other deeply fraught matter of Business Change Management) is fundamental to a core principle of project delivery – that of the contract. The basis of this is that the project team will 'contract' to deliver on time what was promised at the outset, with the resources agreed at that time, *provided* that the third variable, scope, is not changed.

This is a wonderful aspiration, which works well enough as the basis for most projects, and is clearly essential where the delivery is to be done by an external third party who will literally be working to contract. It does however assume two things: i) that what is to be delivered is 100% definable at the outset, and ii) that nothing will change too much during the delivery phase. It could be argued that the purpose of Project Change Management is precisely to manage that second aspect, but as a technique it can only go so far without dominating every discussion of function as design proceeds, and it does rely on condition one being fully satisfied so that the project team can actually detect it is a change in the first place. In reality, Change Management is a tool which should only be used when one of the variables changes in a way which was not, and could not have been, anticipated at the outset.[56]

And that is the issue. In the case of IFPR, one of the three variables was absolutely fixed: the deadline. Unless the system was available by the required date, no amount of good change control or project planning would get over the issue that the business would not be able to start planning for the new season. Some of the functionality was also prescribed: as a minimum, the system had to able to support the planning activities which it would be used for on day one. Resources too were an issue: not because of a shortage of immediately available key skills (which was partially the case), but because we knew that to deliver something like this in such a short timeframe would require the *smallest* possible team, not the largest.

As Fred Brooks says in *The Mythical Man-Month*:

> *'adding extra resources to a late software project simply makes it later.'* [55]

What was accepted is that the scope would 'evolve' or be fully defined not at the beginning of the project, but more probably not until the end. The definition of what was needed would be complete at the same time as the project was.

A few good men (and women)

The idea of using the operating theatre analogy of a 'surgical team' for software development was conceived at IBM in the early 1970s, when the whole business of writing code was hugely labour-intensive. Dr Fred Brooks captures the essence of it in *The Mythical Man-Month*, in which he summarises it as a way of dealing with two big issues:

- communication (the more developers on the project, the bigger the communication problem), and
- productivity (good developers are very, very good. Bad ones are very, very bad).

His ideal team was nine people, the brightest and the best. What some of those people were engaged in has now been replaced by automated tools (and these were also key to the rapid delivery of IFPR), but the principle applies: if you create large teams you will, by definition, have people with a variety of training, experience and capabilities, and if you then reduce them to a set of interchangeable man-days in creating the other big challenge, the project plan, then you have a recipe for disaster.

Project plans

Although it seems counter-intuitive and even (if you're a project manager) heresy to say it, the enemy of rapid delivery is the project plan. All projects need a plan, of course, but the assumptions on which it is constructed and the level of detail need to be carefully thought through.

As a project plan concerns activities which will happen in the future, it is by definition a forecast rather than a certainty. The two key things it needs to define are: what needs to be done, and how long it is going to take to do it.

The first one brings its own challenges, which, again, traditional approaches do little to address. In the world of software development it is usual and perfectly reasonable to break the process down into sequential phases: analysis, design, construction and testing. Each of these can employ well-proven techniques to produce prescribed deliverables, the whole being referred to as a Project Management Methodology. Several well-known versions of these exist, from the so called 'Waterfall' methodologies such as Prince 2[57] – do one phase, then when it is complete (and not before) do the next – to the so-called 'Agile' methodologies, such as the thrillingly titled 'Extreme Programming', which sounds as if it should be an Olympic sport.[58]

The issue is always how to deal with the things you don't yet know about, without at the same time getting stuck in 'analysis paralysis'. All project plans suffer from the 'incompleteness problem', and it is how this problem is dealt with which can make the difference between success and failure.

With IFPR, although it sounds foolhardy to even say it, we didn't have time to create a plan. Or rather we did, but the plan which existed was there to track just the critical milestones, *back-scheduled* from the go-live date. Once again, purists will be rebelling at this heresy: how can a project ever succeed if you plan backwards from the end, rather than forward from the present?

Because of the immovable deadline, this was in reality the only way to create the plan, but it also had the advantage of avoiding the biggest cop-out in normal project planning: the inclusion of contingencies.

Planning backwards

Starting with the end date, it is easy to see what needs to be done and by when: the system needed to be available at the start of September, so it must have passed all possible testing before that date. Testing could actually start as soon as the first iteration of code was available, which the development team believed could be as soon as one week after the project started. It was completely understood and accepted that this code would not work properly, and would not be anything like what was required in terms of screens or functionality, but it had the huge advantage that the London end could look at it and say, '*no, that's not it!*' While they were refining their designs, the next iteration could be produced.

This style of design and development iteration relies on special people: not just generalist analysts, but people who know merchandise planning as well as the planners (who had anyway mostly left); not just programmers, but people who are skilled in using advanced productivity tools (some of which they had to write themselves), and also exceptionally good at generating, understanding and implementing new ideas even when 200 miles apart. The biggest asset on any project is people with knowledge and IFPR had them.

Because of the nature of the team and the iterative approach taken to delivery, the project plan became a tool for managing not tasks and resources, but risks. There was no additional overhead in monitoring and reporting, and tracking simply involved checking to see if we were hitting each (back-scheduled) milestone, and if it looked as though we might miss one, working harder to ensure we didn't.

Nor was there any contingency built into the plan: there could be no time flexibility; taking Fred Brooks' advice, the team size was fixed; and any 'white space' (the normal way of dealing with the unknowns which always plague project planning) was flushed out. Likewise, because there were no tasks, there could be no 'buffers' in the form of *let's allow 10% longer for this or that*' which cautious project managers, who know they will be held to account for late delivery, always include.

Rapid projects challenge everyone who is working on them, particularly the key executive sponsors.[59] It takes a brave management team to give them the freedom to simply get on with it, especially without the comforting, although often false, reassurance of a traditional plan.

Unfortunately, most projects fail

The 2016 Standish CHAOS Report concludes that more than 65% of all projects (by measure of time, scope and budget) fail.[60] That frightening statistic has not changed much during the 20 years the CHAOS report has been produced. Recent high visibility failures of especially public sector projects only underline this, but it is not just governments who mess things up.

Mark Kozak-Holland, in *Titanic Lessons for IT Projects*,[61] quotes some frightening examples of project failures. Others include:

- In 1993, FoxMeyer was a successful, $5 billion company; the fourth largest distributor of pharmaceuticals in the USA. Three years later they filed for bankruptcy, brought down by the largest systems project the company had ever attempted. Giving themselves two years to completely replace the infrastructure on which their entire business depended, they failed to implement anything which got close to replicating what their old, supposedly outdated, systems could do. While the official receiver ('trustee' in the USA) proceeded to sue both SAP (the software provider) and Anderson Consulting (the implementer) for $500 million each (a huge amount, but a fraction of what it had cost FoxMeyer's shareholders), a well-researched study of the whole debacle blamed primarily internal management failures.[62] The company's CIO, Robert Brown, was quoted at the start of the project as saying *'we are betting the company on this'*. Unfortunately he lost.
- In 2005, UK Sainsbury's wrote off £150 million in IT costs after it failed to successfully implement a new automated fulfilment system at its Waltham Point

distribution centre. This was merely one part of a £700 million project to overhaul all of its IT infrastructure which ultimately cost the then CEO, Peter Davis, his job. The incoming CEO, Justin King, did not hold back in laying the blame squarely at the door of the failed IT investment:

> *'It's clear that the major strategic investments we've made in the last three years have not delivered the benefits that we intended. Our automated depots are not fully operational. In July, we announced the need to maintain depots that were planned for closure, but the automated facilities continued to run below the volumes and efficiencies intended. The IT systems that were built to back up that sometimes overcomplicated offer are not yet achieving the targets that were set. And our IT costs make up a greater proportion of our sales than three years ago'.* [63]

- The 'National Programme for the NHS' IT programme was finally abandoned in September 2013. The patient record system would have been the world's largest non-military IT system, but instead became the most catastrophic IT failure ever presided over by a UK government. The total cost was put by the Public Accounts Committee at more than £10 billion, £3.6 billion more than was originally estimated, and it had still delivered nothing. Only 13 NHS trusts out of 169 ever installed the system over the seven years of the project, and for those that did get it, the result was chaos. The Barts NHS Trust lost thousands of patient records, delaying the treatment of urgent cases and costing millions in additional staff time; and the Milton Keynes Foundation Trust wrote a letter to the Times about how bad the system was and cautioning others not to use it.[64]

As we've discussed earlier, these high-profile and expensive disasters do not take into account the likely far greater number of projects which fail *after* the systems have successfully gone live. What is not known is how many of these failures were actually down to flawed project *planning* as opposed to flawed project *management* – i.e. delivery. This might seem like a semantic difference, and is in any case irrelevant after the event, but the perceived and actual role of the project manager is often the key factor which determines success or failure.

Lesson 3: Sometimes standardisation can be taken too far

The final lesson stems from something which we have come across already, and in this case one which only became clear during the years after the project was delivered: namely that implementing a new system creates change in many, often unexpected, ways.

As we saw at Laura Ashley, The Burton Group was implementing not just a new IT system, but also a new business system, both in terms of process and organisation, the full implications of which hadn't been anticipated or properly considered. As we've also seen, the outputs from any new system will always be determined not by the inputs, but by its inherent design, and in the case of the standardisation drive, that was having other consequences.

The standardisation of the data definitions in particular, possibly as much as the process and organisation changes taking place, enabled other decisions (on, for example, the performance of products, stores, and even chains) to be taken for the first time with a far higher degree of confidence.

How to manage the balance between front-of-house differentiation (or else why have multiple brands?) and back-of-house standardisation (or else why have one company?) is a major juggling act which all multi-chain businesses have to master. In the story of Compass Group later, we shall look at one example of how a company seems to have got this right, driven by principles based entirely on economic value. For The Burton Group, however, this proved a difficult balancing act. Often burdened with onerous property leases, and needing to fill the space with something to cover costs, it played over the years with many formats which have now disappeared, including Champion Sport and the Principles brands, but in all cases, as part of a centralised business ethos. The design always focussed on standardisation; but when the same people are buying jeans for several chains, are the ranges going to be that much different? If the same area managers are overseeing different stores, and store design is centralised and (in the interests of cost-saving) emphasising commonality, is the customer experience of the supposedly different stores going to be that distinct?

The project did manage to demonstrate one powerful point, however; often stated as theory, but much more rarely seen in practice: that across businesses of every kind, 75%

of all activities are in fact common; of the remaining, 20% are common across any one sector (such as manufacturing, banking or retail), and only 5% are actually worth tailoring to create what might be a unique, sustainable competitive advantage.[65]

Across the multiple chains of a single fashion retailer such as The Burton Group, where so much was combined, maybe only 1% of everything the company did could in fact be meaningfully different.

Once an organisation gets to that level of homogenisation, the question is: *should* it be different? as it becomes highly debatable whether the disproportionate cost of *any* form of deviation from the norm is worth bearing. While not explicitly stated as such, the answer which prevailed at that time was clearly no.

Note that *standardisation* should not be confused with *simplification*: as we shall see later when discussing Dixons and Compass Group, simplification (or rather the avoidance of complexity) is a mantra which should permeate every decision an organisation makes and a failure to do that can have catastrophic consequences.

A positive outcome of the journey to achieve synergies was that the centralised and now rebuilt (in both credibility as well as skills) Leeds IT department had also moved as far as it was possible to go from the old days: then it had been structured as an internal supplier to its unwilling internal customers, whom it invoiced constantly for its service.[66] MBS was now not *a* supplier, and not even just *the* supplier, but was properly embedded in the business, and its erstwhile customers were now engaged users of its systems.

In contrast to The Burton Group story, we shall look later at the Compass Group/Granada merger in the UK, an example of where standardisation, and the implicit disappearance of everything which one of the companies did, apart from maintaining a brand presence, drove business value. There are, however, many other examples of where bringing together previously separate divisions into one centralised organisation resulted in the destruction of value and ultimately the loss of any expected gains from the process.

One plus one = nothing

McKinsey & Company, the international strategy consultants, reckon that unless any major organisational change delivers at least 10% to either the profits or market value of a company it is not worth doing.[67] They additionally caution against embarking on such a project unless it is also either mandated by some regulatory diktat or very low risk. They suggest that very few projects will pass these hurdles.

Founded in 1982, Compaq rapidly became the world's largest PC manufacturer during the 1990s. Its dominance (and independence) came to an end in 2002 with its opportunistic acquisition by Hewlett-Packard, a mere 20 years after its promising start-up, an event attributed at least in part to distractions and loss of customer focus during its integration and homogenisation of two major acquisitions, Tandem Computers in 1997 and Digital (DEC) in 1998. Sensible though it seemed at the time to diversify into services (which those companies, in contrast to Compaq, had as part of their portfolio; and as many of its competitors were doing in response to falling margins in the increasingly commoditised PC market), it then proceeded to behave as if it had actually acquired two more hardware manufacturing companies. Supposing the synergies would therefore flow from standardising as quickly as possible the operating models of the three PC manufacturers, Compaq basically forgot why they'd bought the other companies in the first place, and in the process threw away any benefit which the burgeoning services arms might bring, as well as forgetting their own key corporate customers. With more than $2 billion of debt on the books at the time of their acquisition by HP, it was a costly mistake.[68]

Interestingly, the take-over (the largest ever deal in the computer industry at that time) didn't cover HP in glory either: they got bogged down in the same issues of trying to extract synergies, and, with the decision to write off $14.5 billion of the $24 billion purchase price immediately, it is still a source of much debate whether anything of real value was achieved.[69] We shall revisit the unfortunate recent history of HP in the next chapter when discussing cultural issues in acquisitions.

Tighten it up until it strips, then back it off a quarter

Attempting to test a theory against a market until it just doesn't work is a risky strategy. The Burton Group's attempt to reduce costs by homogenising every aspect of its multiple brands was a very large-scale example of what many businesses do to a lesser degree all the time – each one relies, however, on the ability to back away from the experiment without doing any lasting damage.

Microsoft was heavily criticised in 2013 when it introduced a new pricing policy for the latest edition of its Office product suite: prior to that it had always been possible to transfer licences from one device to another, but with the latest version, they made that impossible. Once the software (only available as a download and not on a DVD or other media) was installed on a PC, that was it; if you wanted to replace that PC at any time in the future, you had to buy another licence. Users were outraged: after all, they had bought (they thought) a perpetual licence to use the software, and how they then did so (within the legal limits of the agreement) was surely up to them. Suspecting Microsoft of 'gouging' (a term which has been around since the beginning of software licensing for a supplier seeking to maximise its revenue from its customers), they reacted badly, and in the new world of instant social media, made their feelings very publically known. Unfortunately (and this is another feature of such social media) the most negative of the comments were fairly quickly deleted, but it was enough to make even the mighty Microsoft rethink its plans, and allow a transfer to be made once every 90 days.[70]

If a company eventually succeeds with a new concept, however, customers are more than happy to embrace it and forget any previous mishaps. Very few people now remember the ill-fated Apple Newton which was released in 1993 and basically tried to replace a $1 paper notebook with a

$700 computer, but whose core functionality (handwriting recognition) didn't actually work properly. The success of the iPad has overcome any brand damage which Apple might have suffered, even though the concept (and some of the technology) is not a lot different from the Newton. Conversely, McDonald's had to rapidly backtrack on an attempt in 1996 to move to a higher-priced and 'more adult' focussed product range by introducing the Arch Deluxe, a burger which came with lettuce, onions, tomatoes, ketchup, and a mayonnaise-Dijon mustard sauce on a potato bread roll. Its launch was accompanied by an expensive marketing campaign which focussed on the (with hindsight) deeply flawed premise that kids didn't like it so adults should. Not convinced, those adults decided to side with their children (not least because the $2.29 burger replaced the previous $1.90 one), and McDonald's had to hastily withdraw it and replace it with a 55 cent Big Mac to redress the damage.[71] Even though The Burton Group plan might not have been formulated with the explicit intention of changing any front-of-house product, and was based entirely on the philosophy of back-office standardisation, the effect of this was nonetheless experienced by its customers, possibly no less than was McDonald's now long-ditched burger.

And what happened to The Burton Group?

Looking back, was Hoerner's strategy a success or a failure? Opinion is sharply divided, not least between Ralph Halpern, who was scathing about the job he'd done, and

John Hoerner, whose management team Halpern described as 'grey-suited accountants'; however the fact remains that from being worth almost nothing in 1990, it was still around in 2002 when it was bought by Philip Green for £770 million. In 1992, it made a loss of £4.2 million and the share price was 30p; by 1997 it was making a profit of £150 million with a share price of £1.30. For a while the strategy had clearly worked.

At Arcadia, Rose's first job was to massively simplify the group and roll back many of Hoerner's actions. He sold off brands such as Principles, Hawkshead and Racing Green, which Hoerner had bought during the 1990s, and also sold the eponymous store group back to its founder, Robert Wade-Smith, for a total of £9 million. Hoerner had been heavily criticised for paying £17 million for it just three years earlier.

What the company's true value has been over time is difficult to calculate accurately, as the balance sheet has always contained a considerable number of hard-to-value items (including freehold property and long leases, which may or may not be considered as assets depending on their location, and today a pension fund deficit of nearly £1 billion[72]). Recent valuations, however, have put it at around £3.2 billion.[73]

What is true is that Green (or rather his ex-pat wife, Tina, who through her company, Taveta Investments Ltd, is the beneficial owner of 92% of the company) has been paid a considerable amount of money from the business since buying it, including a dividend of £1.2 billion in 2005. Incidentally, that payment was made in a year when the company made a profit of only £253 million on sales of £1.77 billion, and net cash flow was only £404 million.[74]

A fair assessment might be that the work Hoerner did made a huge difference to the short-term survival of the group, but ultimately led to its break-up.

Whether this was inevitable anyway is a moot point: as always with these things, re-organisations move in cycles, and as discussed in an earlier chapter, can be driven simply by change for its own sake (the 'if you are centralised, you need to decentralise; if you are decentralised, to centralise' approach). So, from the highly decentralised, internally fractious business that Halpern had built, Hoerner had created a highly centralised, standardised one, which ultimately proved unsustainable across the different formats.

It is worth noting that with Debenhams now gone, Green seems to have kept many of the Hoerner principles in place for Arcadia, so, if he manages to avoid too much reputational damage from recent events, it will be interesting to see what the future holds.

THE FRENCH CONNECTION

1

Dixons' abortive entry into the new digital age could be summed up by a headline which might have been used many times throughout history when cultures have collided, whether that be the Incas meeting the Spanish Conquistadors or Captain Cook stepping ashore in Hawaii for the second time in 1779 and misreading the apparent friendliness of the natives:

'Old World meets New World – doesn't go well.'

When, in 2007, I joined what I will call Dixons for short (then called DSGi – Dixons Stores Group International – the name as good an indication as any of a company experiencing a crisis of identity), it was about to undergo a seismic change from the ideas of the past to a new, as yet undefined, but hopefully more profitable world. John Clare, with the company for 22 years and Chief Executive for the past 13, was about to retire (an event which some would say was long overdue) and the habits of the past decades were about to be swept away.

Those habits were probably not uncommon in many companies which had been around for a long time and somehow missed the fact that the world outside had changed – managers whose seniority could be measured by the number of ceiling tiles in their offices and the protectiveness of the secretaries stationed outside their doors (currently closed so they could catch up on maybe the latest test match scores with a nice cup of tea[75]) and an overall sense of entitlement to whatever it was that past glories had bestowed on them.

Certainly, the company which comprised Dixons and its other store formats (including Currys and PC World in the UK) had had a long and generally distinguished history, but for the past decade it had been largely living off the cash generated by its late 90s Freeserve[76] adventure. Between 1991 and 2000, buoyed by expansionist spending, sales had grown from £1.7 billion to £7 billion and profits had grown from £82 million to £300 million. More recently, however, growth had stalled and profits had dwindled, and in 2006 the company announced a £200 million restructuring charge against its underperforming European operations, followed in 2007 by four profit warnings in quick succession and a final year loss of £184 million, leading to a 60% drop in the company's share price and an ignominious exit from the FTSE100 index of leading shares.

As well as propping up the old ideas, the Freeserve cash had also been supporting the tired, low-margin formats in the UK. In response to that, the company had tried to enhance earnings growth by expanding into new markets where the business environment was more amenable: some of these had been very successful, as in Norway, where Elkjörp was flourishing in a world with much less competition, and extra-EU trading laws allowed it to conduct what in the UK would have been seen as sharp promotional activity.[77] Others, such as Italy, Greece and Central Europe were performing less well.

Ironically for a company selling many of the new, digital-age products (computers, networking, digital cameras and the like) from optimistically named chains such as PC World, Dixons had never really had a strong or effective presence on the internet, and purely online brands such as Amazon for electronics, and, more recently, Appliances Online for white goods were eating into both its customer base and its already wafer-thin margins. Dixons had to find a way to break into this brave new world, and, ideally at the same time, leapfrog the emerging competition.

It also had to do it without totally cannibalising its own business – trading online in competition with the internet pure-plays had to be done in a way that didn't further erode the margins or undermine the high street or out-of-town stores. A difficult challenge.

The trick, apparently, was to become 'multi-channel', a 'clicks and mortar' retailer.[78]

The first step was to move the struggling Dixons brand purely online. The fragmented, expensive high street estate would become Currys.Digital, an arguably (with hindsight) laughable attempt to rebrand the old-fashioned white goods brand Currys as a new-age player. They would trade out of the usually small-space shops, and stock the usual small-format merchandise, plus maybe a couple of washing machines as space permitted. Consumers, who were used to seeing this product mix in the old-fashioned independent electricals shops which used to be in every town, were clearly even more confused. This confusion was compounded by the Dixons name disappearing into the ether, except in the airports, where they traded as Dixons Tax Free (later amended to Dixons Travel to avoid any ambiguity about what the prices actually represented).

Early problems included how exactly to price the new propositions: Dixons, now entirely online, quite reasonably saw their main competitors as the other online traders, and wanted to price accordingly. This led to some conflict internally, with chains such as PC World and Currys.Digital, burdened with the costs of a physical estate to support, crying foul; particularly as Dixons were selling largely the same product assortment, often with free delivery, but then expecting to utilise the delivery infrastructure (including returns to store) paid for by the other chains.

The biggest problem, however, was that the web technology supporting all this was clunky and performed poorly, and struggled to integrate well, if at all, with the mish-mash of antiquated back-end systems which provided the fulfilment functionality. This was always going to be an issue for the new purely online Dixons brand, even more so than the other chains. The silver bullet to tackle all of this was going to be the acquisition of the French online electronics retailer, Pixmania.

Pixmania, like Dixons itself, had its origins in photography; in this case the family photo printing business Fotovista, which in 2001 was transformed into an innovative online trader by Steve and Jean-Emile Rosenblum, the two sons of the founder. As well as developing their photo storage and printing operation, they had moved into electronics sales, successfully going head to head in mainland Europe with the likes of Amazon, at that time a small player there. They had built a state-of-the-art distribution centre on the outskirts of Paris, from where they shipped small packages across much of Europe, including to the UK. As yet, lacking the physical delivery network required, they had not starting selling any products which couldn't be posted.[79]

A key part of their business model was bespoke software development, and a large percentage of their workforce was dedicated to this task in Paris. The web systems, named e-Merchant, supported by integrated back-end stock systems, were leading-edge and continuously evolving. They contained innovative sales concepts such as dynamic packaging,[80] and an in-house written and populated content management system, dubbed 'Brain', for best presenting the products to be sold. Like rival Amazon's Webstore infrastructure, the system was also available to be used by other retailers, who could outsource fulfilment and sales support to Pixmania too.

For me, Pixmania's business plans had all the glitziness of the best US Silicon Valley dotcom start-ups: they had visionary ideas expressed in the correct new-age language, and aggressive, cash-consuming expansion plans, which (like any self-respecting Silicon Valley business which hopes to be taken seriously) seemed unlikely to deliver any tangible profits in the foreseeable future. Indeed, it is arguable that Steve and Jean-Emile's major selling point could be summed up as: invest to grow, re-invest any and all cash generated (or acquired by any other means) back into the business, and focus simply on the (hopefully growing) company valuation.

All in all, a prospect hard to resist for a poorly informed, cash-strapped but desperate, old-fashioned UK-based dinosaur. What could go wrong?

I joined the business early in 2007, when discussions were well advanced and contracts about to be signed. I had the opportunity to get involved in a little of the due diligence, which threw up a few interesting facts, but momentum was established and the deal was concluded shortly afterwards.

There were going to be three stages to the integration plan: in the short term, Pixmania would get access to the UK stock and distribution operation to expand their product range; in the medium term, Pixmania's web systems would replace the ageing Dixons technology for all the UK brands; and in the longer term this solution would be rolled out across Europe and maybe beyond, with the modern, supposedly low-cost business operations of Pixmania gradually replacing much of what the Dixons brands were currently doing online, while at the same time expanding the range beyond electricals. Through this strategy, Pixmania would enable Dixons to compete with and hopefully become the new Amazon.

Making it happen

Stage one went smoothly enough, achieved on day one by the simple expedient of taking any online orders placed on Pixmania.com for stock which was in the UK, and rekeying them into a store till at head office. Not the most elegant of solutions, but at least it had the benefit of simplicity; and for the UK-based chains, who were starting to view this parvenu competitor with deep suspicion, operationally it was not too much of a distraction.

What it did, though, was open up all the old battles regarding pricing.

Pixmania argued, not unreasonably, that they had to set their prices to compete with the other online retailers in each country, which in the UK meant not just the likes of Amazon (and other smaller retailers starting to use their marketplace as an outlet), but increasingly the new online manifestations of the big supermarkets, such as Tesco.com. This meant that Pixmania was now starting to undercut Dixons.com, who, as we discussed earlier, had just come to an uneasy agreement on comparable pricing with the 'clicks and mortar' chains of Currys and PC World. Every new product and promotion opportunity was fiercely contested, with Pixmania, viewed (at least by John Clare, an approach continued by the new Chief Executive John Browett in a marginally less paternalistic way) much like a young child who needed encouragement even when clearly behaving badly, seemingly being given freer rein and the benefit of the doubt when disputes arose. The fact that Pixmania was relying on the UK warehouses, trucks and staff to actually deliver many of the new products, with the costs simply absorbed into the much larger chains' budgets, did little to diminish this feeling of resentment.

While the dust from this opening skirmish was settling, the main production got under way: the job of replacing the existing websites with the Pixmania technology. And here, as the old and new worlds began to collide, the awesome magnitude of the task started to become apparent.

Despite trading successfully for several years, including operating the back office for another company, Pixmania had never had to make their website work with someone else's systems, never mind ones with so much incomprehensible (and, when it was explained, unjustifiable) complexity. Dixons did have experience of this from the other direction, however, through two equally troubled projects: the work they did to build their new till systems, known as Eclipse, in 2002; and when they had implemented the existing website front ends in 1997. Neither of these projects had ended up covering the participants in glory or delivering what Dixons had hoped for in terms of valuable and sustainable assets, but at least they (after a fashion) worked.

Everything about this work offended the sensibilities of both parties. For Pixmania it went totally against their sense of natural logic and their desire to keep things as simple as possible for themselves. Their line was *'This is what we do, you should do as we say; after all, that is why you bought us, isn't it?'* (answer, yes); *'We know about modern systems. You are dinosaurs'.* For Dixons, the apparent disorganisation and lack of structure generated equally strong frustrations: *'We know how to do structured projects'* (maybe); *'We have a new outsourcing partner to manage who are the ones actually doing the development work*'; '*We're bigger and older so we know better*'; '*We own you*' (after all, we are the ones who have already given you all this money). This stand-off was not helped by Pixmania wanting to charge Dixons for their time, much as they would have done with an external customer, a tactic luckily soon turned off with soft promises of 'we'll sort it all out later'.

As the project unfolded, the reality appeared to be that the majority of the actual work taking place was being done in the UK; the French project manager kept changing, and from the UK perspective, Pixmania appeared to be more occupied with dealing with issues in their own systems than making e-Merchant work with the UK ones.

The greatest challenge of all, however, was trying to understand exactly what was going on. Project meetings were held as often as possible using all available technologies: conference room video links, webcams, shared whiteboards and Skype all played their parts; but it was of course necessary to hold face-to-face meetings as often as possible, and these were invariably in Paris, where the UK participants were inevitably struck by the contrast between their own somewhat dowdy offices in an industrial park on the outskirts of Hemel Hempstead, and Pixmania's swanky location on the Champs-Élysées in the heart of Paris. Far from being the junior partner in the relationship, everything about Pixmania smacked of glitz, success and money. I remember going over to Paris one week to try to unblock some issue or other, and failing to meet Steve Rosenblum as promised. Apparently he had been unexpectedly called away.

The reason was unclear, but while I was sipping my politely offered consolation café, I happened to notice a brochure for the latest Citation executive jet lying on his desk, which may or may not have had something to do with it.

Whatever the reality, and it was always hard to be sure, the project dragged on with no real end in sight. There was much expectation that e-Merchant would go live in the UK at the beginning of 2010. This soon drifted into the autumn and then the following year. Eventually, Currys, PC World and Dixons went live on a much-altered version of e-Merchant in 2013, five full years after the project started. Unfortunately, in business in particular, five years is a very long time, and much had changed in both Dixons' and Pixmania's fortunes. While all this was going on, other, much more pressing issues had been competing for attention: namely the complete divestment of Pixmania; and, in the background, discussions regarding the merger of Dixons with its hitherto arch rival, Carphone Warehouse.

These two events would change everything.

2

The following section is, in direct proportion to the length of time Pixmania continued to remain a subsidiary of Dixons, very short. Unlike in the previous chapters, where the full impact of the decisions the companies had taken only became clear several years later, with Pixmania, it was easy to see that this was going nowhere.

At last, having failed to get Pixmania to make any positive contribution to cashflow or profits, Dixons' patience ran out. A second change of Chief Executive had taken place in just a few years when John Browett (who had succeeded John Clare and then been poached and – if you'll pardon the cheap pun – subsequently roasted by Apple[81]) was replaced by Sebastien James. It seems that he was quickly able to take a much more clear-headed view of the acquisition.

It was also clear that finally managing to integrate the technology had turned out to be a Pyrrhic victory. With Pixmania about to be sold, there was suddenly a whole new issue to be dealt with: the future of e-Merchant in the UK, and the ongoing relationship (fraught at the best of times) with what would now be a completely separate third party company.

The Rosenblums, even when Pixmania was wholly owned by Dixons, had wanted to set up an internal supplier contract for the use and support of the software. As we've seen, however, internal supplier/customer relationships (especially those involving the transfer of money) are inherently flawed, and as a wholly-owned subsidiary of its customer, Pixmania would never have been able to behave (or indeed be treated) as a true supplier, bound by a contract and with appropriate performance guarantees and penalties. As all the assets of Pixmania (including of course the software) were at the end wholly owned by Dixons anyway, any internal licensing arrangement for its use might also have been subject to unfavourable external scrutiny.

Now, however, the issue suddenly became how to unpick all this.

The interim solution was that Dixons would acquire a perpetual licence and the source code for e-Merchant for a one-off payment (undisclosed, but part of the exit deal), and transfer the knowledge on how to support it from Pixmania to Dixons' own staff, thus effecting a complete break from any future relationship.[82] Ironically, while the UK business had been struggling to go live on e-Merchant, unbeknown to them it now appeared that Pixmania had been spending the majority of their resources rewriting the product for their own future use, and this new system went live for Pixmania.com shortly afterwards, leaving the

UK chains as the only users of the supposedly ground-breaking, but now isolated, extremely bespoke and rapidly dating technology. With even more complexity the last thing the newly merged Dixons Carphone needs to deal with, it seems highly likely that the final solution will be that they will throw the whole lot away and use Carphone's much more manageable systems, run by IBM. At the time of writing, the online presence of Dixons.com has already disappeared (replaced by Currys.com), and a new format for Dixonstravel.com has arrived on the scene, bearing a striking resemblance to Carphone's front-end.

Financially – in the end the only true measure of success – the whole adventure was a disaster. Having bought 77% of Pixmania in 2006 for €261 million, and then acquiring the remaining 23% in 2012 for a further €10 million (basically a debt for equity swap to inject much-needed cash, still theoretically valuing the company at €45 million), in 2013 they paid the German venture capitalist Mutares a dowry of €69 million to take it off their hands.

Ultimately Pixmania had proved loss-making during every year of its ownership, and including cash losses and project costs, the total adventure had cost Dixons in excess of €500 million – a sum almost as great as all the money they had made from Freeserve.

3

The lessons learnt from my experience at Dixons (for which I of course was partly responsible) were painful. Armed once again with the benefit of 20/20 hindsight, it should have been clear that with the combination of three critical issues to overcome (technical complexity, as well as corporate and national cultures), this was always going to be a challenging assignment.

Lesson 1: Cultural, as much as technical, problems can sink a merger

It would be tempting to lay all the blame on Dixons' failure to take full advantage of the Pixmania acquisition on cultural differences. On the other hand, this would not be entirely wrong, but the issues in the main were not the expected (and far from uncommon) Anglo-French ones: the real cultural differences were between two companies who had completely different perspectives on what the world of business looked like; different histories and aspirations; and above all different ways of measuring success. In more senses than one they spoke entirely different languages.

As we touched on in the previous chapter, it is an unfortunate fact that most acquisitions fail to achieve their objective of enhancing shareholder value for one reason or another. A review of 2,500 deals over 17 years by L.E.K. Consulting shows that more than 60% of corporate acquisitions actually *destroyed* shareholder value.[83]

A specific example often written about is that of eBay acquiring Skype in 2006 for $2.6 billion. Failing to deliver any synergies at all, or demonstrate any logic behind the acquisition, they had to write off $1.4 billion the following year, and finally sold it in 2009 for $1.2 billion. It was subsequently bought by Microsoft in 2011 for $8.56 billion (an even more extraordinary sum, and at that time its biggest ever acquisition); they too have yet to prove that it has created any real value for them, but at least the purchase served to keep it out of the hands of Google or Facebook, which it was rumoured might have been the real intention in the first place.[84] Interestingly, the ramifications of the deal rumbled on, with a dispute over who actually owns the core technology,[85] an issue which also came up in the Pixmania due diligence.

In another example from the technology sector, HP's acquisition of the UK company Autonomy for $11 billion in 2011 was followed by them having to write off $8.8 billion just the next year, after accusing the directors of fraudulently inflating the company's value, a claim which, at the time of writing (and probably for many years hence) is playing out in the courts. At the same time, HP's shareholders are suing *them* for wasting their money:[86] HP has just offered a $100 million settlement, but this remains to be agreed.

In the next chapter we will look at a company, Compass Group, which has made acquiring and integrating other businesses a core competence and a key part of its growth strategy, but Dixons had little recent experience of this since buying Currys in 1984 and PC World in 1993, and no experience whatsoever of integrating an overseas business.[87]

Acquisitions of French companies by UK ones are comparatively rare; French companies acquiring UK ones are more common. Between 2007 and 2017, there were 10 inward (a French company buying a UK one) transactions of over £100 million, and only two outward ones.[88] This might just be part of the overall (and accelerating) trend of UK companies getting bought rather than buying (a ratio of 2 to 1 between 2010 and 2017, triggering 'UK PLC is for sale' headlines), plus the recent weakness of sterling making UK companies cheap, but the trend predates the effects of recent macro-economic events such as the 2008 crash or Brexit, and might have more to do with the poor track record of UK companies, particularly retailers, overseas.[89] France has always been difficult territory for Anglo-Saxon companies: even the mighty Walmart, expanding everywhere in the world and now in more than 30 countries, has yet to make a play there.[90]

A recent example of an inward acquisition is Accor's €148 million purchase of UK company Onefinestay, described as an 'upmarket Airbnb'.[91] In addition to the purchase price, Accor are reported to be planning to inject another €64 million to develop the business, an act of faith which, interestingly, Dixons did not make with Pixmania. While it is early days, this has many echoes of the Dixons/Pixmania acquisition, but from the other side of the Channel: an old, somewhat traditional company (Accor) wanting to make a leap forward in the world of both the internet and also the emerging 'unhotel' business; the attraction of a small, new-age business whose technology it hopes to integrate; and a way of securing market share in a rapidly changing world. As a similar cross-Channel venture, it will be interesting to see how it goes.

Airbus – a Miracle of Flight

The creation of Airbus and its growth to be one of the world's largest aircraft manufacturers represents the triumph of endeavour and collective will over a multitude of issues: political, financial and, not least, cultural.

The sum total of the distance travelled before assembly of all the individual components in every aircraft produced, legend has it, is greater than the distance the plane itself will travel during its entire working life. The wings are designed and made in the UK, in either Filton near Bristol or Broughton in North Wales, and then shipped (in the case of the A380 wings made in Broughton, *literally* shipped, by barge) to Toulouse; the fuselage is made in Hamburg in Germany, where cabin fit-out is also done (the assembled aircraft is at least flown there) and there is also a plant at Stade producing the vertical tail planes; Getafe in Spain produces parts of the fuselages, horizontal tail planes and also complex composite components; other plants in France make the boxes the wings attach to; and the assembly line where the whole shooting match is finally put together is in Toulouse, where final flight testing also takes place. The entire assembly process covers every Airbus factory in Europe, plus many more component manufacturers: in total around 1,500 businesses in 30 countries. This logistical nightmare pales into insignificance, however, when compared to the problems which need to be overcome before anything is actually made; that of coordinating the design.

Situated in Toulouse, 'Le Plateau' is the headquarters of the central design team, which, for the massive triple-decked A380, consisted of more than 1,000 staff. There were also separate design teams in the UK, Germany and Spain, in all totalling more than 1,400 people. All of them needed to be able to work on and ultimately agree a final design which would enable every one of the four million individual parts which go into a single A380 to fit and work together. It is a colossal undertaking.

In 2003, during a year of study at Cranfield University, I took part in a project to look at how information was shared between all these disparate sites, nationalities and, of course, cultures during the design of the A380, and the results were fascinating.

'Knowledge Management' (KM) became the latest business buzz-word in the early 1990s, with a movement led by the Japanese.[92] Originally described as 'the process of applying a systematic approach to the capture, structuring, management, and dissemination of knowledge throughout an organisation to work faster, reuse best practices, and reduce costly rework from project to project', it rapidly became the new, new thing for management consultants everywhere. Although frequently hijacked by those from the 'soft sciences' school of management consultancy (armed with sales pitches such as 'your employees are your greatest assets; they know everything about how your company works, then walk out of the door'), like so many other ideas, KM is nonetheless routed in hard science; in this case industrial design and especially CAD/CAM (Computer Aided Design and Manufacturing), which since the 1970s has rapidly become the standard way of developing and mass-producing virtually everything. Indeed the history of CAD/CAM is the history of human technological development in the late 20th century, as without it, the ability to make reliably, cheaply and repeatedly many of the products we take for granted (whether that be computer chips, Lego bricks, or indeed modern aircraft) would not be possible; and the development of CAD's 3D capabilities is the direct forerunner of current computer-based animation and gaming technologies, including Computer Generated Imagery (CGI), as well as healthcare breakthroughs such as MRI and CT scanning.[93]

The holy grail of Knowledge Management is the ability to capture not just the 'what' (which is the role of CAD/CAM), but also the 'how'; in other words, the thinking behind the decisions, and the expertise which goes into making them; somehow codifying the minds of the experts doing the job. This has now developed into the field of Artificial Intelligence (AI), a whole other area of study, where the focus has shifted from trying to capture the intelligence of *people* (maybe, it appears, an ultimately futile job) to getting *machine*s to do the learning (from people initially, then themselves) and thereby hopefully develop new forms of knowledge.[94] The new technology here is CD/CM, without the 'A's – in other words, products designed and built by computers alone.

The Cranfield project team was tasked with looking at how knowledge was shared within the Design to Cost (D2C) departments. These are offshoots of the main engineering team, seen sometimes by the designers from their lofty positions on Le Plateau as the poor country cousins (and viewed with somewhat the same suspicion as auditors, who are sometimes described as people who come along after the battle is over and bayonet the wounded), but actually the job they do is vital in enabling Airbus to actually make money. Their role is to consider the finished designs before they are committed to production and basically work out how to do it cheaper, and there is a department based in each of the design centres in Spain, France, Germany and the UK. I led the Cranfield project team in Toulouse, and as well as having the privilege of being able to witness first-hand the final assembly of the aircraft and at the same time sample the local wines and cuisine (being Toulouse, always duck), I was also able to observe how the D2C teams communicated with the Plateau and each other.

And the first shock was that they didn't.

Nor did the designers across the centres, working (don't

forget) on a single, albeit hugely complex end-product. No, each team had their own systems, processes and individual approaches, and only worked on the bit which was down to them. If your job is to design a wing (which the UK team would argue is the most important and only really interesting part of any aircraft anyway), then that is what you designed. How the rest of the aircraft worked, or indeed, beyond a limited set of parameters, how your wing is attached to it isn't of any real interest. Things as diverse but nonetheless important as the engines (simply bolt them on later to your superbly designed mounts), or, at the other extreme, the toilets (as far away from airframe design as you can get, but incredibly important if you're a young designer straight out of college, or that other distant consideration, a passenger) are an irrelevance.[95]

The way Airbus got round this potentially fatal issue was by working hard to define what they called 'systems interfaces'. These were the essential glue which ensured everything worked together, and were to be found in every aspect of the work: technical definitions and standards which everyone worked to; specifications for joints from both ends; precise designs for how the end of the part one designer was working on would fit with the part another was responsible for; precise weight and balance requirements for each component; and also processes. And they were written in multiple languages, both national and engineering. Although the original operating principles of Airbus, set up and implemented by Roger Béteille in the 1970s, was that the standard language would be English and measurements would be imperial, not metric, these were not universally applied and indeed would have been impossible given the origins and histories of the different parties. The 'standard language' might have been English, but in reality very few of the designers or engineers in Toulouse spoke it well, if at all. As we found on the project, it was usually easier to hold meetings in French, or indeed, Spanish, the native tongue of one of the project members and the language of a much closer country than England. Some words used to describe the KM processes did not, we found, even have sensible English translations. Following the long tradition of aviation everywhere, which still uses both metric and imperial measures ('we're cruising at 35,000 feet, with an airspeed of 500 knots'; fuel is measured in imperial gallons, US gallons or litres, then, depending on what type of instrumentation you have, it has to be converted to either imperial pounds or kilos for weight and balance calculations), many drawings were in both English and French, and had scales in both millimetres and inches.[96]

If all this was difficult for Airbus, who had been working at it for many years, it was no wonder it challenged Dixons. What was undeniable, however, was that Airbus eventually produced aeroplanes which flew, unlike the Dixons/Pixmania design, which, for a long time, didn't.

France is a foreign country, they do things differently there

Any discussion of cultural differences would be incomplete without touching on the thorny and difficult subject of *national* cultures and particularly the challenges facing British and French companies when they work together.

This is dangerous territory; there is a huge risk of falling back on the usual national (or worse still, nationalistic) stereotypes in order to explain or excuse poor working relationships and failed outcomes. It is however an issue, and one better acknowledged than ignored. Much has already been written on the subject; most of it not very scientific, and quite a lot in the cringingly awful 'how to do business with the jolly foreigners' genre of business advice. The more serious authors tend (quite rightly) to concentrate on technical matters such as the legal and regulatory environments, banking, and corporate structures, and only briefly touch on what they sometimes describe euphemistically as 'business etiquette' (which is, of course, one of those enigmatic French words which doesn't translate well into English[97]). Even then, this is usually limited to trying to explain to confused Brits and Americans that in France it is not considered rude to be late for meetings (although very rude to try to hold an unplanned one), that people will often stray off the agenda, and that it is over lunch that the real work is done.[98]

Having had some early exposure to transnational working at Laura Ashley, albeit with the culturally pretty similar Dutch, I had gained much more experience of working with other European nationalities at Tonka, and then worldwide with Compass Group. In all those years, I had to work much harder at understanding the challenges of doing business in France than anywhere else. Pixmania may have been what the French call a 'start-up minded' company, but in many ways it had the same traditional attributes as any other Gallic enterprise. Over the years, many people have tried to give me advice, and I've taken counsel too from as much reputable writing as possible, but nothing can quite prepare you for the cultural differences in practice. To quote randomly from some of these sources:

- *'Cross-level working is often not effective'.*
- *'French leaders are often charismatic and articulate. Decisions are made at the top and should not be questioned'.*
- *'People involved are not always consulted prior to the decision-making process. To work effectively you should:*
  - *make sure that you have a large internal network to find out what exactly is going on within the organisation*
  - *frequently socialise with colleagues, e.g. by having lunch*
  - *in case of virtual communication make sure you call the people you work with on a regular basis'.*
- *'A good leader or superior gives his subordinates clear instructions. Assignments and job descriptions should be well defined.'*
- *'The French excel in debating so interrupting in the conversation is permitted as it is seen as taking on an active role. They often refer to their well-known philosophers to anchor their thoughts and ideas when giving business presentations.'*
- *'An area of tension may occur when French people speak English and keep to the French structure. The structure of the French language may suggest, when speaking in English, that one is making a statement or giving instructions,*

however this is usually not the case. It often causes irritation and misunderstandings.'

- *'Meetings are not always structured. One of the challenges is a difference in thinking styles; the French are deductive thinkers. They often focus on the "why" when others focus on the "what" and "how".'*

- *'The French enjoy a good intellectual monologue or debate during meetings. Being articulate is seen as having had a good education.'*

- *"Yes' rarely means yes in the way British people understand it – it more often means something like, 'I hear your argument (which I will now proceed to demolish with my impeccable logic as I don't agree with it)'.'*

All these issues come to a head in the Project Meeting, and the problems can occur anywhere in what is often characterised as Southern, Mediterranean or Catholic (to distinguish it from Northern, by implication cold, Protestant) Europe. I remember doing a project with a business based in Palma, Mallorca; as pleasing a location as you could wish for to hold monthly progress review meetings. As the representative of the corporate centre, my role was to offer support and also provide oversight to what was, for a small company with little experience of these things, a major IT replacement project. We needn't go into the details of what happened, but I remember the meetings well. Mallorca is a reasonably long flight time from the UK, so it was not possible to get there and back in one day; I would therefore fly out the previous afternoon, to be met by the local management team and treated to an always enjoyable evening of tapas and wine, followed (much later) by dinner.[99] A not-too-early start the following morning would involve getting picked up from my hotel at around 9 o'clock (a time at which in the USA they would just have been wrapping up the now almost obligatory 'breakfast meeting') and taken for a leisurely coffee at a local bar. Having sipped that and put the world to rights (never a word about business or the project), we would go into the office for the meeting which was due to start at 11.

Several days before the meeting I would always check that the usual preparations had been made (minutes from the last meeting circulated; actions updated; the project report made available; a new agenda issued including timings so that everything could be covered, especially as I had a plane to catch immediately afterwards) and that the Spanish project manager was happy with progress on everything to date (he always was), and was prepared to provide an update and answer questions from the key stakeholders. The reality every time was completely different. By the time everyone had arrived, shaken hands and sat down (the CEO, as most senior participant, always last) and coffee had been served, often half an hour had passed of the two which had been scheduled. To give everyone credit, there was then always a game attempt to stick to the structure and content of the agenda which all parties had so compliantly agreed, but this usually lasted for no more than 10 minutes, after which the meeting always went the same way. People would start, often simultaneously, talking about the issues most important to them, which was usually how badly everything was going;

this would then escalate into animated shouting matches, with people standing up and waving their arms at each other in (for a north European) an extremely disconcerting manner, and the carefully structured meeting would disintegrate into a free-for-all. After maybe 20 minutes of this, the shouting would stop; everyone would smile and shake hands (once more the best of friends); and the most senior people would make their apologies and leave, followed shortly afterwards by everyone else.

It was only after several months of this that I realised what was going on. The reality was that the project was actually being progressed in the way they always did things: by informal relationships and much airing of views by the coffee machine, and either the generation of a common consensus in the team, or unquestioned formal direction from the CEO. The monthly review meetings, which I saw as such an important event, but which were from their perspective completely peripheral, were being staged entirely for my benefit.

Once I had worked this out we stopped this time- and money-wasting exercise and at first it was extremely difficult for me. Eventually it was replaced by less regular (but no less frequent) visits, where we did almost exactly the same things as before, but without the charade of the formal meeting. I learnt more about how the project was really progressing, and was probably able to help much more effectively in providing support and direction and resolving blockages. Or so, with their infinite politeness, they had me believe.

Lesson 2: You can't buy simplicity

One of the key issues Dixons faced was the sheer complexity of its back-office systems. These had evolved over many years, and rather than tackle the problem at its source, each successive challenge had been met by building a new solution and bolting it onto what was already there. By 2007, the number of individual software systems exceeded 200, running on an equally large number of hardware platforms of all types and ages. Physical business configurations (e.g. regional warehouses) were each supported by their own system, all surrounding a creaking old mainframe which no-one dared to touch. Indeed the number of programmers *in the world* able to work on it was rapidly diminishing as they aged, retired, or passed away. Dixons employed six of them, possibly 50% of the world's available expertise.

This strategy of adding on rather than replacing or modifying was not in response to a technical challenge, but to an organisational one. IT had never been positioned effectively within the structure of the business (or respected enough) to be listened to when issues of increasing complexity had been raised, and a lack of organisational will had scuppered any attempts to address it, despite the rising costs. The eventual decision to outsource much of the legacy IT was taken in the fond hope that, by writing it into contracts and making it someone else's problem, the cost would finally be brought back under control, but of course it did nothing to address the underlying problem, of which the escalating cost base was merely a symptom.

This unwillingness to address the organisational

issues was at the heart of not just the complexity in the IT infrastructure, but in the business itself. Unlike at The Burton Group in the previous chapter, where one or other business model (highly centralised and standardised, or decentralised individual trading divisions) had very clearly prevailed and been enforced at any one time, at Dixons it was not at all clear what the rules were, and no-one had sought to clarify them for many years. While many of the back-office functions appeared to be shared (for example, finance and HR), in reality the trading divisions, through the straightforward expedient of simply doing it, had also managed to retain their own internal capabilities in those areas as well as many others. The resulting duplication, differences (often simply for the sake of being different or retaining a power base rather than for genuine business reasons) and compromises which this had created were the reason the business had become as fragmented and high-cost as it had. How to tackle this was by no means clear, and an attempt to standardise as well as modernise the company through a new systems replacement project (dubbed more in hope than expectation 'One Group') was abandoned as the almost unsurmountable difficulties of possibly this last opportunity became apparent.

Not everyone can be easyJet

I joined Dixons after spending some time as IT Director at easyJet, and the cultural shock was immense. Although not a case study here (and much has already been written and much is taught in business schools about the easyJet story[100]), I learnt many powerful lessons from my time there, the biggest of which was that if you want to be a truly low-cost business, you have to have the basic principles of simplicity in place from the very start. However hard you might try, you can't take a high-cost company and magically become low-cost, or think that it's just a matter of doing things differently.

Many companies, including other airlines, have tried to achieve that goal. British Airways, for example, in an attempt to fend off the challenge from easyJet (early life motto: '*Kill BA!*') created a spin-off in the 'low-cost' mould called Go Fly. Started in 1998, it survived for a while before ultimately being bought in 2002 for £374 million by its erstwhile competitor (largely for its slots and assets in the form of 27 aircraft and 3 major UK bases), after failing to make a profit. Similarly, Buzz was acquired from KLM by Ryanair in 2003, and SAS abandoned its low-cost experiment, the unfortunately (and amusingly) named Snowflake.

While having many of the replicable attributes essential for low-cost airline operations (such as direct sales, single leg point-to-point journeys, high aircraft utilisation through speedy turnaround times, and multiple bases where aircraft and pilots could spend the night at home rather than in expensive foreign destinations), what Go Fly appeared to fundamentally lack was the necessary internal culture which easyJet had: a total rejection of the accepted norms and cost structures inherent in traditional airline operations, and most importantly, a mindset that no vested interests would stand in the way of it achieving its aims. As a wholly owned subsidiary of BA, this was always going to be hard to achieve, and Stelios Haji-Ioannou, the larger-than-life founder of easyJet, would also accuse BA of illegally subsidising its offspring's operations directly or indirectly, an accusation which they steadfastly denied and later defended in court.[101]

Despite its ultimate sale, it had still managed to grow its passenger numbers to 2.7 million, many of which it had acquired from its parent BA; one of the facts which hastened its sale, firstly to 3i and the management, then to easyJet.[102]

Where's the money?

Nothing would have benefited Dixons more than being able to adopt the principles of a low-cost business. Margins in electrical retailing are extremely thin and this flows all the way from the initial purchase price. Most of the more desirable products are branded, and the power rests firmly with the supplier, whether Apple, Sony or Miele. Own-label products can be a way round that, but despite often performing well in consumer tests, they do not attract a price premium in the shops and are expensive to produce in limited numbers. Lower-price items (e.g. Beko from Turkey, or Servis, branded as a British product, but also Turkish-owned now) can have potentially slightly higher gross margins, but starting from a lower price point. Dixons' fulfilment infrastructure was also undoubtedly complex. Some of this was a consequence of the product they are selling, but much was not. They had a huge central warehouse in Newark for store replenishment (at the time of opening in 2006 the largest container park in the UK, and during the stock build-up to Christmas as busy as Heathrow airport), plus a dozen or more Local Distribution Centres (LDCs) dotted around the country designed to support home deliveries. Stock could be in any one of those, ideally placed close to the customers for easy delivery, but this wasn't always the case, so products could be delivered from a nearby LDC or from the central warehouse, sometimes via the LDC. Fulfilment was further complicated by the nature of the product: some items could be delivered by one person, some (such as large fridge-freezers or washing machines) required two. Delivery might also include the installation of, for example, a gas cooker, requiring a certified installer to attend as part of the delivery. All-in-all, electricals is a difficult business to make much money out of.

Pixmania appeared to offer a different business model: the sales process was largely automated, as was warehousing; and delivery was outsourced to the postal service. What was not clear at the outset, however, was the extent to which the true mindset of low-cost was embedded in the culture of the business.

Outsourcing

At the same time as it was acquiring Pixmania, Dixons had also played what it thought was its other get-out-of-jail-free card, and was in the process of outsourcing its entire legacy IT infrastructure to an Indian company, HCL.[103]

Similarly ill-informed and ill-prepared for the consequences of another such momentous decision, struck (like a similar one with BT) for short-term balance sheet management reasons, Dixons was then faced with the prospect of managing not one but two parties to achieve the desired result. While HCL was in no way to blame for the resulting failure to integrate Pixmania, 100% occupied as they were trying to get to grips with the cumbersome beast they had taken on, their presence added a further complexity, again as much cultural as technical, to the process.

Apart from the multi-national aspects, the clash of cultures was being further exacerbated by the conflict between the demands of a formal outsourced development process at the Dixons end (specifications, estimates, sign-offs, and structured methodologies; all part and parcel of managing an outsourced relationship) and the highly informal (iterative, prototyping-based, unstructured – even, as it was perceived, chaotic) in-house development process in France.

Outsourcing and low-cost speed to market are not mutually incompatible ideas however; much of easyJet's success is based on the philosophy that outsourcing can be an effective enabler of agility and a source of competitive advantage. easyJet's outsourcing strategy, however, is based on two quite distinct concepts: outsource non-core commodity activities, and outsource to the passenger.

The first of these is self-evident, but with a twist: easyJet has been highly successful in outsourcing commodity activities where the activity wouldn't initially have been seen as a commodity. It does this by creating genuinely contestable markets where markets did not previously exist. Well documented examples are baggage and passenger handling (previously jealously guarded monopolies at many airports); 100% available IT infrastructure (the innovative contract signed with Savvis in 2006); and most famously the breaking of the Swissair monopoly on *everything* at Geneva in 1999, which ultimately led to the resident flag carrier's bankruptcy in 2002.[104] We shall discuss this more in the next chapter.

The second point is more subtle, but equally important – easyJet outsources every aspect of the business that it can to its *customers*: the booking process; online check-in for themselves and any baggage they have; boarding card printing; bag drops; self-check-in kiosks and booking changes.

What makes this possible was its ability from the outset to use sophisticated (though simple), integrated and innovative information technology, exploiting the power of the internet and more recently its logical extension, cloud computing. When a passenger buys a ticket, checks in or prints a boarding card, they are interacting directly with easyJet's own internal systems. There is no intermediate process or person involved: the passenger is doing exactly the same thing as a call-centre sales assistant or airport check-in clerk would be doing, they're just doing it themselves, on their computers or mobile phones, at home or on the move. To the customer, the website easyJet.com, plastered all over the planes from 2005, *is* easyJet.

This deceptively simple activity, which provides a seamless customer experience and is essential for achieving lowest cost of operations, is actually very hard to do, and was proving virtually impossible for Dixons. Not that long ago, before the new till system was installed, web orders, having been placed online by a customer, would actually be manually re-keyed into a till system in head office; leading to errors, delay and often rework as it transpired a product wasn't available or a payment failed or it was simply miskeyed. Even with the supposedly integrated web system, there was no immediate online authorisation of payments, and a degree of rework if a customer's payment card or credit application subsequently failed. As we've mentioned, this approach was unearthed for the first phase of Pixmania's integration.

It is important to point out that this wasn't a problem Dixons was alone in facing: in the early days of e-commerce, IT departments, who for decades had been the firewall (for both good and bad) between business users and the IT systems, could not cope with the new model where the general public, rather than captive, manageable internal staff, were becoming the users of what they saw as *their* systems. These new users were demanding, intolerant of failure or poor performance, and wholly unpredictable in their behaviour. Accessing the systems from computers which were outside the control of the over-controlling IT department, they also brought new previously unaddressed challenges to old-fashioned security and data integrity models.

The IT department's response was often to install intermediate systems: there were tales of supposedly new digital services being installed which at the front end looked swish enough, but behind the scenes consisted of a printer (or in one instance, a fax) which then allowed a human to rekey the data into the existing systems.[105]

Where's the stock?

Web-based systems, which allow this new class of users (i.e. a business's customers) direct access to a company's internal data bring their own problems. Especially, it brings into sharp focus the need for real-time data accuracy, a lack of which, up until then, companies could to a degree tolerate. In an earlier chapter we saw how Laura Ashley had had to fix problems with the roll lengths of its fabrics once internal sales were being counted: once stock is being sold directly to customers online, the problem suddenly becomes exponentially more urgent.

This need for 100% accuracy of real-time inventory was not a new one for every sector of course. Back in the world of airlines, they have their own inventory system: in this case, seats. The accurate tracking of the availability (and price) of that inventory is what generates an airline's income. When a new season goes on sale, easyJet might be selling 40 million seats at a rate of several hundred *a second*, and, following the rules in its Yield Management system, changing their prices constantly. The inability to track seat availability would be unthinkable.

IBM runs what they used to call 'usability labs', now positioned as part of their User Centered Design (UCD) practice.[106] Over the years (like much in IBM, which tends not to shout about its best things) this has been quietly innovating new approaches to design and testing software systems.

Usability design and testing, as opposed to theoretical design or the other related topic, Human Computer Interface (HCI) design, started well before computers were in common use. Human Factors[107] as a discipline began during the Second World War as a way of understanding the interaction between people and machines. It has long been recognised that the way people behave when they interact with machines, processes and systems can be radically different from what might be anticipated; again, the Law of Unintended Consequences comes into play.

In the 1980s IBM did some work with Ford Europe, who were about to roll out a new computerised stock control system to all their wholly-owned and franchised service agents across the continent. It would be replacing the old, manual microfiche and ledger-based systems which had been in place almost since the birth of the company. The users would be the parts department managers and staff whose job it was to serve on the one hand the general public who came into the garage for spares for their cars, and on the other, the internal service department of the garage. As this would be a major change for these frequently traditionally-minded people who had little or no experience of computer systems, Ford (sensibly as it turned out) decided to engage IBM to help.

In order to assess how the usability tests had gone and enable more detailed analysis afterwards, IBM would, as well as making real-time observations, record the whole process with video cameras covering the physical environment and the people involved, and also tracking what was on the computer screens. The recording of the first test of the new system was revealing, and the result completely unexpected.

The parts store was set up in the simplest possible way: on a shelf behind the counter (labelled 'Shelf 1') was one single box, containing an oil filter for a 1966 Ford Cortina Mk I (labelled 'Part 1'); the computer system stock file was loaded with the single part and its location, and all was ready to go. A customer comes into the garage and the cameras roll:

Cast:

CUSTOMER – Joe Bloggs, car owner and DIY maintenance
 enthusiast
PARTS ASSISTANT – a real Ford parts department
 manager, clad in obligatory long brown coat

(CUSTOMER enters parts department)

CUSTOMER:	'I'm looking for an oil filter for a 1966 Cortina Mk I – do you by any chance have one?'
PARTS ASSISTANT:	'Let me have a look for you, just give me a minute.'

(PARTS ASSISTANT turns to the brand-new computer system and looks up the part.)

A screen comes up showing that, yes, the part existed, and the garage had exactly one in stock and it was on the shelf behind him. Everyone observing the test (Ford managers, software developers, IBM support staff) is at this stage holding their breath in eager anticipation of a successful result, when:

(PARTS ASSISTANT looks up from the computer screen and turns to the customer)

PARTS ASSISTANT: 'Sorry, mate, we're completely sold out.'

Cue total panic from everyone involved, and a sudden and shuddering halt to the test. What on earth had gone wrong? Why, when the system showed that the part was in stock, and where it was, did the parts assistant say there wasn't one?

And the answer which emerged would transform Ford Europe; because on being asked why on earth he had said what he'd said to the customer, the parts manager replied:

PARTS ASSISTANT: 'Oh, we never sell the last one in stock in case the service department needs it.'

When they extrapolated that apparently simple statement to every single product in every single parts location across Europe, Ford calculated that the total cost of unused (and unsaleable) stock which they were carrying as an unnecessary overhead came to nearly £300 million, and this revelation changed their stock management policy overnight.

Dixons had somewhat the opposite problem when it came to implementing their Collect at Store strategy: here, stock frequently proved to be *lower* than expected, manifesting itself as a huge customer service issue when a product had been 'reserved' online, but was not actually there when the customer travelled to their local shop to collect it. Fortunately, Dixons had not implemented a system whereby the customer had to pay for the product *before* collection, a path which some other retailers decided to follow later, with mixed results, but even so, it was not a good outcome.

The issue in this case was that 'stock' could include products that were never going to be (intentionally or otherwise) sold to the customer: items which were on display (and which may or may not have been saleable); damaged goods; and products which were simply missing but had not yet been recorded as such. In some cases, it was because of a timing issue, and the only available product had just been sold to another customer before the shop had received and actioned the instruction to reserve it.

In order to compensate for this, the systems were modified to allow for a margin of error, and initially at least, a shop wasn't shown as having *any* available stock at all unless at least three were listed on the stock file. Again, a huge wasted opportunity and potential for unsaleable stock to be carried, but at least not a customer relations disaster. The equivalent would be like easyJet, which sells 75 million 'products' – i.e. seats – every year, having an extra few seats in every plane on the off-chance that when the passenger boarded, there wasn't a spare one available. The reality, as many people know to their cost, is the exact opposite, in that many airlines (though, until recently, not easyJet)[108] are so keen to maximise the income from their fixed, highly perishable inventory that they overbook flights knowing (and hoping) that not everyone will actually turn up. This would be like Dixons selling (and taking a non-refundable payment for) more products than they actually have to customers online, knowing that in reality *not all them will turn up to collect them*!

Lesson 3: Never forget what business you are in and how the money is made

At one point in *Breaking Bad*, Walter White says:

> *'Jesse, you asked me if I was in the meth business or the money business. Neither. I'm in the empire business.'*[109]

It may be that, by buying a business apparently so radically different from what it was used to running, Dixons temporarily forgot the fundamentals of what it should have known best: how to make money out of electricals. No matter what the future opportunity might have been, Dixons' expectation (rightly or wrongly) was that Pixmania would, as well as doing all the exciting things promised before its acquisition, make an actual positive contribution to the bottom line. It is an unfortunate fact, however, that this expectation was completely at odds with the plans Pixmania themselves had, and diametrically opposed to the development curves of virtually all new-age internet companies.

It takes money to make money

On May 15, 1997, a loss-making online bookshop floated on the Nasdaq exchange in New York in an IPO which valued it at $438 million. Twenty years later, that start-up, called Amazon.com, is worth nearly $460 *billion*. What is most amazing is that for almost none of those twenty years did it make any money; even though it had grown to be the largest and most influential online retailer in the world, up until 2016 it had never made a profit. Valued in 2016 at 115 times earnings (even when there started being any), this was a monumental act of faith by its investors. It has never paid a dividend, and even when total sales were topping $100 billion, every one of those dollars was either absorbed by costs, or, more importantly, ploughed back into the company as further investment, a total of more than $60 billion to date. It took Amazon 18 years as a public company to catch Walmart in market capitalisation, but only two more years to double it. If an investor had put $1000 in Amazon when it floated, that investment would now (taking three stock splits into account) be worth $64,000 in May 2017.[110]

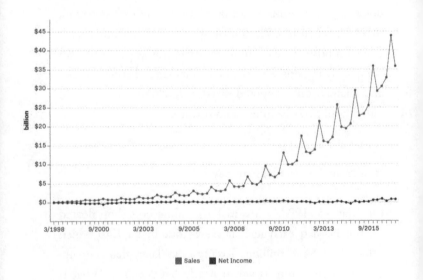

Amazon: Sales and Profits

What is most frightening (for other retailers) about this new Amazon is that, at the same time as starting to deliver profits, they have also dropped their discount positioning. They no longer have to advertise all products as 'x% off' on their website to make a sale; now they simply state the price the customer will pay, and it is up to them (if they so choose, and clearly many do not) to compare prices and make the decision whether to buy. This has not dented sales in the slightest; in fact, in the first quarter of 2016–2017, sales were up 23%. Part of this transformation is their new focus on excellent customer service. Their 'Prime' offering, while appearing to focus on speed and value for delivery, is also a huge boost to free cash flow: delivery payments are made up to a year in advance; and, taken together with supplier payment terms of 30 days *after the customer sale* (the stock cost in effect still being carried by the supplier until then), further increase its ability to generate huge amounts of cash. Commentators are predicting that as the new model develops, operating margins, which used to be solidly negative, will approach 10–12%; an incredible result.[111]

As well as failing to appreciate the amount of cash which Pixmania might require to make it into what it aspired to be, Dixons also undoubtedly lost sight of what was its core business. We've mentioned before the mistake Compaq Computers made when they acquired Digital Equipment in 1998: at the time Michael Dell, of Dell Computers, was quoted as saying: '*I gotta believe that these guys have just handed us a huge gift*'.[112] He was referring to the distraction that integrating this new player would cause for Compaq, and as we have seen, he was right, with Compaq falling into

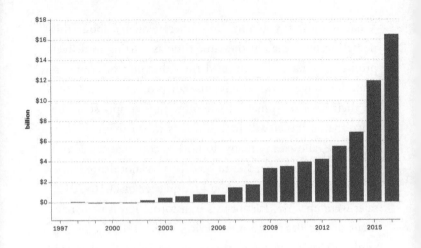

Amazon: operating cash flow

the hands of arch rival HP a mere four years later. History is littered with other such examples:

- For business school students, the failed Daimler-Benz Chrysler merger is probably the one most studied. Much as in the Pixmania story, its demise can be blamed almost completely on its inability to overcome entirely predictable cultural issues, which over the 10 years from 1998 which the deal took to unravel, cost the Chrysler shareholders more than $28 billion.[113] So much effort was spent on trying to extract the supposed synergies (which, again with the benefit of 20/20 hindsight, were never actually there) that they forgot that their prime objective was to sell vehicles. One issue which emerged was the pay differentials between senior managers in the two companies. At the time of the merger, executives in Chrysler became rich as stock options triggered: that against a background where the Americans were already taking home three or even four times the Germans in pay.[114] The main reason why this was not seen a merger of equals however was not about pay, but about management style. It became clear very quickly that Daimler-Benz was calling the shots: large numbers of Chrysler senior managers left within two years of the merger, and most telling, by the time of the sale only 8% of the merged company's shares were held by Americans. The biggest impact of all this distraction was on Chrysler's US sales, turning an operating profit of $10 billion into a loss of $1.5 billion over the same period.

• Novell's acquisition of Cambridge Technology Partners (CTP) in 2001 is sometimes cited as the beginning of the end for what was once the dominant networking products company. As a purveyor of the industry leading Netware software, Novell was not really equipped to deal with the consultancy-focussed business of CTP. As the new CEO, Ron Hosvepian, said in 2006, '*we confused our sales model with our business model. We started selling consulting, when we should have been using consulting to sell our software products*'.[115] This was a perceptive observation; customers had trusted Novell to sell reliable enterprise networking software and were thrown by the shift of direction. They viewed with suspicion the new consultants on the block and left in droves for Microsoft, who at least had never confused the issue by trying to be overly helpful. Novell tried many things to regain its market position, but it was finally bought, first by Attachmate and then in 2014 by Micro Focus; its value by now largely residing in a collection of nearly 900 patents which Novell had spent the last few years fiercely fighting over (rather than selling software). The acquisition neatly brought the patent disputes to an end by the straightforward mechanism of the previous litigants (Microsoft, Oracle, Apple and EMC) buying them.[116]

I once had the pleasure of attending a seminar by Eileen Shapiro, author of *Fad Surfing in the Boardroom*.[117] A fun seminar (and a fun book); she said she would start by telling any of us who were thinking of doing a Harvard MBA how to save the then projected cost of more than $100,000. 'I'll sum up the entire course for you in five words,' she said, '*don't run out of cash.*' It is easy to criticise Dixons for temporarily forgetting the basic principles of a business they should have understood, but maybe they could be forgiven (as a mature business) for misunderstanding the completely different cycle of internet start-ups. Although times were tough, fundamentally Dixons did know how to sell electricals. Conversely, no amount of cash can compensate for a lack of basic business knowledge, and there is no better illustration of this than the story of Webvan:

- Founded in the heady days of the late 1990s as an online local grocery delivery business, Webvan attracted almost overnight nearly $400 million in investment from eager venture capitalists who had been left traumatised (and, as they saw it, substantially poorer than they should have been) by missing out on some of the great success stories of the previous 20 years. These had included Silicon Graphics, Jim Clark's 1982 start-up which, in its heyday, was turning over £3.7 billion. Clark left in 1994 and immediately co-founded Netscape, which went from zero to a valuation of $1 billion in just 17 months. In *The New New Thing*, Michael Lewis tells the amusing story of Alex Slusky, a young venture capitalist who was assigned to sleep under Clark's bed so that he could be the first one on the spot if he woke up with another new idea.[118] Webvan had no trouble therefore getting funding: what it lacked was anyone who had the slightest experience of any of the things it was planning to do. Seen as fundamentally an 'internet company' (whatever that was), at its core it was still a grocery retailing and delivery business; apart from having a new store front, not really very much different from the corner store and boy-on-a-bike businesses which had been around for the last 100 years. The new CEO, George Shaheen, left a $4 million a year job at Anderson Consulting (now Accenture) to head it up, but had no experience of the grocery business. He brought in a management team also seemingly lacking any relevant experience, and after attracting an IPO valuation of $6 billion (when the company had revenues of just $5 million), Webvan went bust in 2001 having spent more than $830 million in just two years.

That does not mean that 'focussing on your core business' means only doing one thing. Adam Hartung wrote an interesting and provocatively titled article in Forbes[119] pointing out that many technology companies have succeeded *because* they have broadened their focus, while others have struggled because they didn't. In *Stop Focussing on Your Core Business*, he points out that Apple entered 2000 dedicated to the Macintosh and almost bankrupt, but after spreading its wings to include new products, often far-removed from its traditional base, including iPods, iTunes, iPhones, and iPads (and more recently services such as Apple Store, Apple Music and Apple Pay), it is now one of the richest companies in the world, with cash reserves in excess of $250 billion.

And finally…

Unlike many of the internet start-ups of the time, such as Facebook, Google and the like, who had to work out completely new business models which could deliver a profit, at the end of the day, Pixmania was essentially an electronics retailer, albeit one with a new kind of storefront, and the fundamentals of the business model should have been no different.

The failure of Comet in 2012 helped bolster Dixons' sales for another year. Bought the previous year by OpCapita for £2, the private equity firm had failed to turn the 240-store business round, and Comet closed its doors for the last time in the November of that year, having changed the face of UK electricals retailing forever in the 1960s by being the first truly discount trader.[120] Ironically, in 1989 Kingfisher (the then owner of Comet) had made a hostile takeover bid for Dixons, an approach which was successfully rebuffed by Stanley Kalms, Dixons' chairman, who referred the bid to the Monopolies and Mergers Commission. The MMC concluded that although the combined high street presence of the merged businesses (Currys, Dixons and Comet) would be below the key threshold of 25% market share, it would still be significantly greater than the next nearest competitor, Rumbelows (shortly afterwards also defunct), and, more importantly, would give the new group nearly 80% of the rapidly growing and much more profitable out-of-town market, the reason why Comet had wanted to buy Dixons in the first place.

In 2014 Dixons finally completed its merger with Carphone Warehouse, creating a new FTSE100 company, Dixons Carphone, worth at the time of the merger £3.4 billion. Carphone Warehouse had themselves been handed a temporary lifeline by the recent failure of Phones4u, caused by the network operators one by one pulling out of having any relationship with them as they came to see it as a competitor (and not a very nice one at that), which was not only undercutting them, but also undermining the brand value they had been trying so hard to develop. It is at the time of writing unclear why the relationship with what is now Dixons Carphone could not ultimately go the same way. Indeed, at the time of the merger, EE threatened to do exactly that, but have so far remained with them.

After peaking in value in 2015, this new entity, in March 2017, repeated DSGi's feat of exactly 10 years previously by dropping out of the FTSE100. With the increasing dominance of the online traders (particularly Amazon), the trading model and back-end infrastructure of Dixons only partly resolved, and the mobile network operators more and more re-establishing their own retail presence on the high street and thus reclaiming Carphone's traditional customer base, it will take all the energy and expertise of the new Chief Executive to ensure its future survival.

THE WEDDING PLANNER

1

Compass Group is probably one of the largest UK-based companies most people have never heard of. At around number 20 in the FTSE100, it has a market capitalisation of £25 billion.[121] In terms of its operations, the numbers are impressive: it employs more than half a million people in around 50 countries worldwide, feeds nearly 15 million people every single day and serves about 5 billion meals a year in its more than 50,000 foodservice outlets.[122] Very few of these are to be found on the high street,[123] but are situated in locations where people work, travel, or go for education, sport or entertainment; what Compass Group calls a 'semi-captive' market. It operates well-known franchised brands such as Burger King, Dunkin' Donuts and Harry Ramsden, plus its own in-house developed brands such as Café Ritazza and Upper Crust, and trades under a number of industry-specific identities, including Eurest for Business and Industry worldwide, Canteen for Vending Services in the US, and Restaurant Associates for corporate in-house fine-dining.[124] If in the past 12 months you've had lunch at work, eaten at a sporting event, had a meal while waiting for a train or a plane or braved the food in a hospital as a visitor or a patient, then it is quite likely that you will have been served by some part of Compass Group.

Compass operates various different business models through which it makes a profit from its operations: from simple retailing (rent a location, sell food at a price people will pay); through retail concessions (sell food but pay usually a percentage of the proceeds as rent to the site owner, often a railway station or an airport); to 'fixed-price' or 'cost-plus' contracts (sell food to a firm's employees at a price set by the employer,[125] pass on the costs of food and labour and be paid a subsidy which becomes in effect the profit[126]), usually to corporate business and industry clients. In all cases, profitability relies on the ability to negotiate the purchase and delivery to the unit of basic ingredients at the lowest possible cost, plus manage in the most efficient manner the back-office of what is, at the coal face, a highly labour-intensive operation.

The largest growth spurt happened during the 1990s after its management buy-out from the leisure, drinks and property conglomerate Grand Metropolitan in 1987 and public listing in 1988, when it expanded from being a mainly UK business to operating in over 50 countries. This expansion was driven by the acquisitions in rapid succession of Scandinavian Service Partner (the ex-Scandinavian Airlines airport concessions business which was merged with the already owned ex-British Rail railway station caterer,

Travellers' Fare, to create Select Service Partner – SSP), Canteen Corporation in the US (business and industry foodservice plus the world's largest vending machine operator) and Eurest International (from Accor[127]), giving it a global reach in employee feeding.

Acquisition is usually a strategy for increasing market share, but can also be a vehicle for eliminating a competitor or gaining access to a prized asset (a contract, customer, property – intellectual or physical – or equipment). Whatever the reason, acquisition as a strategy for growth (as opposed to 'organic' growth, or 'selling more' as it is more commonly described outside business management schools) is, as we've already seen, fraught with risk. Suddenly owning a largely unknown quantity (pre-acquisition due diligence only being able to go so far), whether the identified synergies (another key buzzword) can be delivered, and whether at the end of the day the whole will turn out to be greater or less than the sum of the parts, all remain to be seen.

Compass had thought about this very hard. As well as gaining market share, at every stage of the expansion a simple principle underpinned the acquisitions: could it further leverage its two core economic drivers of food purchasing and operational efficiency to increase shareholder value? If this was the case, it may be that an acquisition could be earnings-enhancing from day one, even if the company being bought had previously been loss-making. In some cases, this turnaround could be achieved by the simple mechanism of combining the purchasing catalogues of both companies: increasing the volumes and hence supplier discounts or rebates, and at the same time ratcheting the price down to the lowest of the two currently being enjoyed by either company. The bigger the acquisition, the bigger the reward: the larger the purchasing volume being acquired, the greater the benefit.

I joined the business in 1996, at the start of what was to be an intensive period of delivering on that promise. SSP and Canteen had just been added to the fold, and in the middle of a strategic review of how we were going to integrate them, the problem suddenly got many times more complex with the acquisition of Eurest.

This review had been a major investment for the newly divisionalised company, involving senior managers (almost exclusively from finance, it has to be said), mainly from the group centre, the UK and the USA, with outside help from management consultants Deloitte and Touche (as it was then, now simply Deloitte). The review had tasked itself with basically selecting two common IT packages, one for deployment in each of the foodservice units, and one centrally for finance, billing, and general administration. The intention was that these would become the standard way of doing business, and that this in turn would be the mechanism for creating a unified group. And that is indeed how the project started.

Modernisation and standardisation

During the period from 1996–2000, the back-office systems in the UK and USA were replaced with industry-standard platforms, modernising them from the mish-mash of disparate systems which the business had grown up with over the last few decades. In the UK, that meant replacing central purchasing and billing systems, which were in some cases more than 30 years old, and in the US it included consolidating 65 separate locations into one processing centre and creating the first complete asset register of the some 100,000 vending machines. At a restaurant level, standard systems replaced the myriad of disparate devices, many of which were simple electromechanical tills with no ability to do other administration functions, track stock or even communicate outside the unit. At every stage, the commercial logic was to standardise the back-office (billing, purchasing, finance and payroll), and to enable the individual foodservice outlets to deliver the lowest cost service. As these outlets can range in size from a café operated by two people, to the busiest Burger King in the world employing 140 people in Schiphol Airport, and in the Business and Industry division included the task of feeding every one of IBM's 400,000 employees worldwide, this was no simple task.

Although hard work and a huge project, none of this was in itself very remarkable; the systems needed replacing, and the impending year 2000 uncertainty (a very useful 'burning platform' argument, as we discussed earlier) added a small but useful urgency to the timing. What *was* unusual, however, was the single-minded focus on delivering value where value existed to be delivered, and using the systems to drive simplicity rather than add complexity.

Most importantly, some critical lessons were learnt along the way, the most important of which was about the degree of homogenisation which was appropriate for what was rapidly becoming a very large multinational organisation. There were three aspects to this: two surrounding what 'common systems' actually meant, and the other about data and process.

Any colour as long as it's black

The two IT solutions chosen were, for the foodservice units themselves, a PC-based product called ReMACS, developed in California and already well established in the USA; and for the central processes, a German-engineered software product called SAP,[128] one of the two market-leading multi-national providers at the time of what, in the trade, are known as Enterprise Resource Planning (ERP) Systems.[129] It was assumed before the project got underway that simply selecting and implementing these common packages would achieve the desired result of unifying the group; once the work started in earnest, however, it quickly became clear that this wouldn't necessarily be the case.

Unfortunate facts about the other acquired businesses also began to emerge and start to muddy this hitherto tidy strategy. Both France and Australia, countries which came into the group as part of Eurest International's sprawling empire, were already users of Oracle, SAP's bitter rival, and the one which had been rejected by Compass Group in the selection process. While neither of these businesses were of the scale of the UK or USA, if the strategy was to be properly applied, shouldn't these two countries also switch to SAP? Finally, the question underpinning what had so far been largely an act of faith had to be addressed: what was the overall benefit (other than neatness) of having a common IT solution, and was this benefit sufficiently large that it justified imposing a system which, had that country been looking for a new stand-alone package, for reasons of cost or complexity might not actually have even figured on the shortlist at all? Moreover, was this benefit sufficiently large that it also justified the cost of throwing away and replacing an already installed, working solution?

Once it was put in those terms, the answer was clearly no. The initial implementation approach was also put to the test (and ultimately the sword) when two other countries, Germany and the Netherlands, announced that they were also planning to replace their own systems. Largely for the purpose of benefiting from a group-negotiated licensing deal, and also keen to be seen as team players as well as taking the route of least resistance (there was considerable pressure from the corporate centre), both agreed that indeed SAP would be a perfectly good solution. The process of deciding how to implement these systems, however, was fraught with difficulties and tested a further key (and so far not addressed) issue, that of organisational design. A proposal was put forward to leverage the investment the UK had already made in what was, after all, a multi-national solution by using their system and IT infrastructure, and setting the UK division up as an arms-length service provider to their European colleagues. Despite further (although increasingly less strong) support from the corporate centre, the plan was rejected by both parties to the prospective arrangement, the UK and in this case the Netherlands.

The project in Holland took me back (in many ways) to my time there with Laura Ashley. Ten years earlier I had enjoyed working with the generously hospitable but often blunt-speaking Dutch. Once again, I experienced both: the former in the shape of very early (usually 11.30am) and entirely dairy-product-based (cheese, milk and yoghurt) working lunches; and the latter in the form of the particularly straight-talking Dutch Finance Director (who was sponsoring the project) as he explained in his extremely fluent but heavily accented English the reasons why he didn't want to participate in any pan-European collaboration: '*No way*,' he said, '*it will be scheet.*'

Plat du jour: les systems régionaux

The problems with the in-unit restaurant systems were of an entirely different kind. The chosen solution had already been well-proven in the hospitality market in the USA, and it had been felt that being able to deploy this in other countries would not only give Compass Group the required (but again not really very well defined) benefits of standardisation, but might also, as a uniquely-licensed product, give the sales teams a competitive edge (and source of additional revenue) in selling Business and Industry catering contracts. In the 'cost-plus' businesses, this was an 'extra' which, as well as providing functionality clearly essential to the smooth-running of the operation, would hopefully also be paid for (at 'cost', with of course some 'plus') by the client. The fact that the competition did not have access to it, and there was therefore no contestable market to drive prices down, would prove beneficial on both fronts.

The reality was again very different. Whereas SAP was a package already designed (at great cost) to operate in an international environment, ReMACS was not. Creating such a solution is no trivial task: to be truly global, the system has to be multi-*everything*, including language, currency, accounting standards (of which more later), legal framework (for example, apparently simple things like what an invoice has to contain is different in every country) and even the rendering of text (SAP includes many non-Roman scripts, including Arabic, Japanese and Cyrillic), and must seamlessly operate in any one, or indeed all of them at the same time. It must also be designed so that it can be configured in flight without any new coding, and maintain its transnational integrity during software upgrades. SAP has an annual Research and Development budget of $3 billion.[130] ReMACS, on the other hand, had a total annual company turnover of less than $20 million, of which precisely zero had so far been spent on internationalisation. It was no wonder then that the first stage of the deployment outside of the USA, adapting it for use in the UK, would ultimately be unsuccessful and it was concluded ReMACS would only be used in its home market.[131]

You say potato and I say tomato

The final area was data and reporting. Much like the IFPR project at The Burton Group, the project started with the expectation (at least amongst the control freaks at head office – finance and, more surprisingly, marketing) that it would lay out a common set of definitions that could be used globally. This would consist of a common worldwide financial Chart of Accounts, plus standard coding and data definitions for products and clients. In addition, management reporting would be standardised to enable a common (and central) view to be taken of the performance of business units at every level. This immediately came up against some fundamental issues, not least of which was that, outside the corporate headquarters, no-one wanted to do it. Practical questions too quickly started to intervene in this utopian vision; Compass Group was by now a multi-national business, and in other parts of the world, they really do do things differently.

Cutting a not very long story even shorter (largely so as not to embarrass the participants too much), the project was pretty quickly abandoned in favour of using a simple consolidation approach to generate the numbers for head office, much as every other similar international company in the UK had been doing for some time. While the ERP solution, SAP, had the ability to perform this consolidation itself, to achieve that it relied on every single entity across the world using it, which was of course why the SAP sales team were pushing this capability so strongly in the first place. It is interesting to note that SAP's largest rival in the Enterprise Software world, Oracle, finally admitted defeat in this area by acquiring in 2007 the industry-leading provider of data consolidation software, and the one which Compass Group eventually chose for group reporting, Hyperion. As for client data, it was decided that only where clients were operating in more than one country and (this is the important bit) where those clients actually *wanted* to be treated as a single entity (usually they didn't), would information be consolidated so that global reporting could be done.

From the intentions at the outset, by the end of what was a four-year project, much had changed. Practicalities had replaced theory, and the process of implementing what had started out as an Information Systems project had forced Compass Group to also think about data and process, and ultimately about organisation. The company had created a solid strategic foundation which would now stand it in good stead when it embarked on its most audacious, complex and city-baffling corporate play, the merger-acquisition-flotation-demerger-sale of the collected assets of its UK business and those of Granada PLC in 2000.[132]

An arranged marriage… err, and divorce… or something (possibly)

The deal, which hit the headlines of the financial press at the time, reunited the original and later much-elevated protagonists from the group's management buyout from Grand Metropolitan in 1987: then CEO of Granada Contract Services, later of Granada PLC, Chairman of the Arts Council and now Sir, Gerry Robinson; at the time Finance Director of Compass Services and later CEO of Compass Group, also now Sir, Francis Mackay; and Charles Allen, then CEO of Granada, who went on to run Granada

Media and later ITV, and now Lord, Baron Allen of Kensington. The whole complex transaction was rumoured to have been dreamt up and fully planned out over one, or more likely several, late-night dinners.

The upside from Granada's viewpoint was that, once all the moves had played out, they would end up as a debt-free pure play media company[133] (and avoid a huge Capital Gains Tax bill by floating rather than being sold off from Granada Compass), while Compass would double the turnover of their UK foodservice operations, again while avoiding building up any debt on the balance sheet – the whole shooting match, with hindsight, a clever play which at the time completely foxed the financial analysts in the city who had not spotted the end game until too late.

Once the dust had settled, and while Andrew Lynch, the Compass Group Finance Director, was busy selling the ex-Granada Forte hotels to pay off the debts,[134] both of which had come with the deal from Granada, the integration team started the job of looking at the two UK foodservice businesses. The motorway service stations would fold nicely into the Compass SSP business and would (with the objective of distancing itself from the more negative aspects of its historical reputation) be rebranded from Granada Services to Moto; the big task however was how to integrate the two contract foodservice arms, which had almost identical and therefore duplicated organisations. A team was put together, and, from my role of Group CIO and armed with the experience of other Compass mergers, I was seconded to the UK division to look at the systems and processes and recommend a way forward.

Coincidentally, the IT systems of both organisations were almost identical: replaced at about the same time for broadly similar reasons, both companies now ran a version of the same system, SAP. This fact had immediate attractions for the management of the new business: surely we could simply take the best of both, combine the assets and get an additional benefit rather than a cost for the integration? There was an expectation that this process would be simple: both companies used the same system, so surely they were all but integrated already?

The result of the review, performed using the same principles as all of Compass Group's other integration projects and also applying the learning gained during the previous four years of the Group IS Project, was, to the new UK (ex-Granada) MD and his management team, surprising. Yes, both companies used the same system for the same fundamental processes – client invoicing, the central purchasing catalogue, finance, payroll, and management information – but the way the two companies did this was very different. The way SAP (as we've discussed, a highly flexible system in terms of configuration options during installation) handled these processes was therefore also completely different. A more woolly-minded company may have tried to gloss over these fundamental issues and, for short-term reasons and what they would have thought of as an easy option, as well as avoiding the need to deal with any asset write-offs, might well have stuck with two (bungled together) versions of SAP running the combined business. Compass Group however, applying its principles of simplicity and the experience of previous mergers, was amenable to an alternative scenario: instead of attempting to combine the two back offices, systems and processes using an amalgam of what was already there, it made far more sense to keep just one of them, train the other businesses' staff to use it, convert the data, and simply throw the other one away.

With hindsight, this sounds like an easy conclusion to reach and the obvious decision to take, and because of the work done to demonstrate this option, so it proved. What made it so unusual, however, is that it is highly unlikely that very many other companies would have done the same thing. What helped enormously was the need to combine the purchasing catalogues as quickly as possible and to decide what to do about the two back-office accounting centres and other support services. Having selected the business model which was to be retained in terms of processes, reporting and IT systems (those of Compass Group as it happened, but the benefits were marginal and it could have gone either way), those decisions were straightforward and their implementation could proceed at speed and with confidence.

The project took 12 months to complete, at the end of which the back offices of both companies had been combined into a single integrated UK operation running just one system, with minimal impact on the front-of-house service delivery. Including the combination of the purchasing catalogues, it would go on to deliver £70 million in bottom line benefits in the following year.

3

Observant readers will have noticed the absence of a Section 2. Unlike in the previous chapters, in this case study there is no unfortunate aftermath to be reported. Indeed, like all good weddings where the couple are well-matched and have thought properly about what they are doing, the marriage proceeded well. That doesn't mean that there weren't any lessons to be learnt however; there were, and some very important ones. The difference was that Compass Group had managed to learn (and apply) them as it went along, thereby avoiding the kind of post-project fallout which afflicted the companies which we've examined previously. That is not to say that all these lessons were recognised as such at the time, or that their application was always pain-free, but, whether by good design or simply good fortune, the outcome was successful and the effect on the group entirely positive.

Lesson 1: Decisions about data and process are also decisions about organisational design

Although Compass wasn't thinking about it in those terms at the time, what it was doing in defining how data and processes would flow through the organisation, in particular the levels of consolidation and standardisation, was at the same time defining its future organisational structure. As we've discussed before in the Laura Ashley example, such decisions can have profound consequences for the future well-being of an organisation, but decisions about process and data can often be taken in the heat of an IT project by well-meaning but relatively junior analysts without any real thought or understanding of the consequences. Luckily for Compass, it was already going through a period of profound change, and was in a mindset where it was able to stand back and consider these issues at the right level. It probably surprised itself at the outcome. It certainly led to a new style of management, moving away from a hands-on, somewhat micro-managing past, to a more delegated and trusting approach. It laid down the principles about the size (and relative autonomy) of operating divisions, spans of control and delegation of responsibilities. Those previous control freaks (largely but not exclusively in finance and marketing, and many of whom had recently been elevated to group-wide roles from positions in the UK) had to either adapt, or in the case of some senior managers, move on.

A global chart of accounts? Common systems?

The attempt to create an international group standard Chart of Accounts was particularly instructive. The UK has a set of accounting standards, collectively known as GAAP (Generally Accepted Accounting Practice) which governs how companies should report their results. They are highly technical and constantly changing, and being up to speed with the latest FRS[135] something or other is the *sine qua non* for every self-respecting UK accountant. They are of course not the same as the US GAAP, neither of which are quite the same as IFRS (International Financial Reporting Standards), which is an independent, non-governmental agency, supposedly supported by the G20 and all major financial institutions, whose mission it is to produce a harmonised code for international financial reporting.[136] Except that the US are reluctant to adopt it, which is somewhat undermining its admirable ambition at present. Around 10 years ago, converting companies to IFRS became the new buzzthing for management consultancies everywhere hoping to make a quick buck out of a long, slow project, but in reality, often because of the underlying difficulties with IT systems as much as anything else, not a lot of progress was made. Undeterred, where IFRS were fearing to tread, Compass Group launched in with both feet. Driven by the above-mentioned desire for control by the corporate finance team (led by the then Group Finance Director, Roger Matthews[137] and his Group Financial Controller), they issued a set of guidelines which went well beyond the needs of corporate reporting, and was basically a Group Chart of Management Accounts, to be completed by the trading divisions on a monthly basis, and consisting of information which drilled well down in the performance of the smallest parts of the overseas operations. Rebellion ensued: 'who was running the business anyway?' 'What's it got to do with you?' were common (if not loudly spoken) questions.

I remember well visits to the US for review meetings. Charlotte, North Carolina, headquarters of Compass Group's North American division, was my most frequent long-haul destination in a role which meant spending a large amount of time travelling.[138] After a long flight, it felt almost like a homecoming to check in at the modest Wyndham Gardens hotel just across from the office, and come down from dumping my bag in my room to find the barman had already placed a wonderfully cool bottle of Sam Adams Boston Lager on the counter for me. After eight hours in the air, at what felt like midnight UK time (because it was!), but was actually 7pm local time, it tasted like heaven.

What became abundantly clear very quickly was that the team in the US, under strong direction from their then CFO (now North American CEO) Gary Green, wasn't that interested in participating in (or, more specifically, contributing to) any group-centric project, but merely wanted to do what would offer most benefit to their new, increasingly independent division. Looking back, it should have been obvious that the economics of human behaviour were being played out in the only way they could be, by the participants following the direction set not by the theories of the Group IS Project, but by the hard numbers dictated by their incentive schemes, which were geared entirely to delivering the local results. The benefits of the project had never been fully explained in terms of how the local division, as opposed to the corporate centre, or that even more nebulous thing, the overall 'group', would share in the spoils, nor had this been spelled out in terms of achieving their personal rewards.

The power struggle was fought subtly, as all the best ones are, and often found expression in criticism by the US team of the new management of the UK division (they, of course, being the old team) rather than the group centre. Discussions ostensibly about reporting standards and common definitions were in reality a proxy war about reporting lines and spheres of responsibility. I knew this was not going to be an easy ride when I presented (as the representative for Roger Matthews; when I joined, my boss) the proposal for common divisional reporting, and the North American Division CIO, as representative of his boss and US CFO, just laughed.

The urgency of coming to an agreement was highlighted by the need to make some fundamental decisions about the ERP systems which were about to be implemented in both the USA and the UK. It is an inescapable fact that, as part of the initial configuration of SAP, fundamental decisions about organisational and data structures need to be made which will subsequently have a profound effect on how the system (and therefore the organisation) works, and the sudden realisation of that can come as a shock to any company which has not given it enough thought in advance. Indeed, the whole project should be put on hold until the questions are answered, an unfortunate fact which has caused more than one organisation to panic and for the purposes of maintaining momentum, simply invent a structure it later came to deeply regret.[139] At Compass Group, it was very instructive (and somewhat entertaining) to sit in on an early design session in the USA and hear a junior SAP configuration analyst from IBM (the chosen implementation partner) ask innocently 'so, tell me what the top level company is?'. The two options were clearly either Compass Group, as in the corporate centre, where the top level chart of accounts would then forever reside, or Compass Group North America, which would immediately define the division as a logically separate organisation. '*Compass Group North America*', was the immediate answer from the North American CIO, and through that simple statement the future management structure of the entire group was determined.

As it happens, and whether this was by design or an instinct for independence (OK, it was the latter) doesn't really matter: it was almost certainly the right decision. As we have seen many times, decisions on organisation can have an enormous impact, and implementing Enterprise Systems can fossilise these in such a way that it is impossible to unpick them later without spending a great deal of time and money. Remember one of the most important lessons from System Dynamics? 'The outputs of a system are conditioned not by the inputs, but by its design, and that is impossible to overcome.' This is particularly true when that design is embedded in a system such as SAP, where the processes and rules are rigorously enforced, and no change, however small, can be made to any part of the organisational structure without it having an effect somewhere else.

The degree to which an IT system can hard-wire an organisation's structure and processes (and even its management behaviours) is rarely acknowledged and not well understood, and, despite the existence of some well-publicised but probably not very well attended to case studies, it is still happening with alarming regularity. SAP in particular, probably the most flexible and configurable of the ERP systems out there, once actually configured becomes as flexible as concrete. In the case of Compass UK and Granada, both had chosen SAP, but the decisions they had made about how to configure it had hard-wired the two businesses in entirely different ways. The more globally integrated the system, and the greater the span of control they cover in a single 'instance' (the technical term for installation), the more they hard-wire EVERYTHING! The biggest issue then comes when the system needs to be changed for whatever reason (maybe something as small as a new regulatory requirement in some subsidiary): being fully aware as we are now of the law of unintended consequences, this clearly needs to be very carefully thought through indeed, and the amount of time (and therefore money) this can take also needs to have been (but almost certainly wasn't) part of the original business case.

A house of many parts (most of them flawed)

A particularly problematic effect of this is what happens when companies then proceed to outsource their IT systems, as Dixons had done in 2006. These kind of outsourcing contracts (for reasons of being able to measure their performance) are typically based on maintenance of the status quo, usually with cost-saving targets built in. This is all well and good if what is being outsourced is well designed and already able to fully support the changing needs of the business, but it rarely is, else why outsource it? Occasionally such an arrangement has value in preserving and ultimately winding down a legacy environment so that other resources can concentrate on replacing it with something else, but if this is not part of the plan what the company is doing is perpetuating the hard-wiring, often for many years to come.

As we've discussed before, if what is implemented has been explicitly designed to produce the results you want, all well and good, but if it has not, then beware. In an article for the Harvard Business Review, Donald Marchand and Joe Peppard compare a typical IT systems environment to the mansion built in San Jose, California by Sarah Winchester, widow of the gun magnate, which she started in 1884 and worked on continuously until her death in 1922.[140] Not wanting to use an architect, she designed every aspect of the house herself, including 40 bedrooms, 47 fireplaces (but only 17 chimneys), and most famously 10,000 panes of glass, including one specially designed by Tiffany & Company to cast a rainbow across the room. Unfortunately it was installed on an interior wall with no access to natural light. An extreme, if diverting, analogy, you may be thinking, but a house with doors which go nowhere and windows which look out only onto walls is exactly what you will create (and have to live with for many years) if you configure your wonderful new ERP system in haste. While Mrs Winchester may have been able to afford to pander to her eccentric whims and construct something which owed more to the etchings of MC Escher than rational practicalities, most businesses can't and shouldn't.

More examples of how legacy processes embedded in ancient IT systems can constrain and ultimately threaten a business come from the world of banking. In *Competitive Strategy*, Michael Porter describes three generic strategies: differentiation, cost leadership and focus,[141] and until the internet came along, these were the accepted ways of ensuring long-term corporate survival. Facing threats from new 'digital' competitors who could short-circuit the often laborious relationship between a business and its traditional customers, banks in particular have been slow to respond. Differentiation takes on a new meaning when services need to be delivered digitally: having an online presence, a highly functional phone app, and the ability for your customers to transact their business anywhere at any time, stop being sources of competitive advantage and become simple necessities. Any financial organisation which can't do that as a minimum differentiates themselves only in a negative sense. It is notable that many traditional businesses are finding this transition difficult, and cost leadership (never a key area for inherently high-cost banks, who are after all funding themselves with someone else's money) becomes reinterpreted as the cost of the customer's time rather than lowest-price product. In a world where one-click, on-the-move interaction with nearly every other consumer business is rapidly becoming the norm, it now seems incredibly antiquated (and annoyingly time-wasting) if you have to ring someone up, for example, to renew an insurance policy.[142]

Another example is the way in which new entrants are taking traditional business models apart by applying what used to be called 'disintermediation': putting buyers directly in touch with sellers for services, in some cases entirely new ones, as well as products. Excellent examples are Airbnb and Uber, the former starting a whole new 'unhotel' industry involving people renting out rooms or whole properties where before they might not have even considered this, as they had no easy mechanism to accomplish it. Likewise, Uber, along with similar 'platforms' (in the new lingo) such as Deliveroo, are introducing new business models which are challenging even traditional and hitherto well-established things such as the relationship (as well as the legal rights) of employees, employers and customers.[143]

All of these examples (and there are many more) throw down a huge challenge to existing incumbents, not because they couldn't enter those markets themselves if they wanted to, but because the whole DNA of the organisations concerned is often so embedded in legacy ways of working (in their systems in the widest sense) that to do so would mean throwing away almost everything which (at least they and presumably also their shareholders believe) gives the company value today. This is an incredibly high-risk strategy: in common with the new entrants, there is much to gain, but unlike for them, there is also much to lose. We have already seen how traditional airlines attempted to defend themselves against the new low-cost, internet-enabled entrants such as easyJet by attempting to start their own versions, only for them all to fall by the wayside one way or another, possibly because, ultimately, their parent companies could not have allowed them to succeed, as doing so would have inevitably involved destroying what they had spent years building up themselves.

Redefining the role of the centre

Back at Compass Group, as these dramas played out in the divisions, the nature of the corporate centre was changing too: previously pretty much indistinguishable from the UK business (for a time they shared the same accommodation and it was almost entirely staffed by ex-UK senior managers), it was now faced with having to define its new role in the massively enlarged group. It responded by firstly moving to separate premises situated in Chertsey on the outskirts of London (the UK business was based in Hammersmith, 15 miles away), then preceding to both slim down, and also recruit new, external staff who would start to perform these new 'group' roles. These had included myself in the new role of Group IS Director,[144] plus a new Group Purchasing Director, neither of which positions had any direct reports. The previous Group Marketing Director role was migrated to one dealing mainly with corporate communications, and a new department for supporting the rapidly growing portfolio of global brands was created. The thorny issue of who should be the sales lead for international clients (and there was a satisfyingly growing number of these too, including IBM, Philips, Microsoft and Ford Motor Company) was resolved by giving it to the most appropriate division (e.g. the USA for IBM and Microsoft); recognising that that was where the experience, competence and key contacts sat, not in some far-off corporate centre, however much it might have wanted to own (and control) the process.

Information too now flowed into the centre through the newly defined processes of consolidation and arms-length reporting, not through totally integrated databases designed so that, for example, someone in group finance could drill down into the detailed performance of a unit anywhere in the world, which was what had been initially envisaged. Only summary information now made its way out of the divisions, where it was finally accepted that the responsibility for managing performance actually sat.

Compass had come to realise that any other solution, as well as potentially incurring huge costs for little return, would actually *prevent* the proper delegation of responsibilities and thereby ultimately constrain rather than facilitate the growth of the group.

Lesson 2: For the last time (I promise) – Mergers are Difficult!

We've come across the thorny issue of mergers and acquisitions and how to make them work many times throughout this book, and there is no better place to briefly summarise and then conclude this topic than when discussing Compass Group. We've seen how often mergers go wrong – and amazingly they seem to go the most wrong when they involve two businesses which should be the most similar.

Q: When is a pound not a pound? A: When it's 99p

The US acquisition by Dollar Tree of its larger rival Family Dollar in 2015 for $9.2 billion[145] and the remarkably similar (although far smaller) £55 million acquisition by UK Poundland of its erstwhile rival 99p Stores the following year are recent cases in point. Whatever it is about discount retailers, in both cases the merger of two outwardly identical businesses clearly caused an unbelievable amount of mayhem. Following an ultimately successful bidding war with rival Dollar General, the US merger created a mega-chain of more than 13,000 stores, but Dollar Tree seemed to get bogged down for some two years in trying to make the deal work (it had already taken over a year to obtain shareholder and regulatory approval and actually complete the paperwork) and only returned to earnings growth some time later.

The terms of the transaction specified by the Federal Trade Commission (FTC) included the condition that the newly combined business needed to sell off 330 of its stores to avoid charges of the merger being anti-competitive, and as this activity had to be completed within 150 days it certainly consumed some of the time, but it does not explain the huge amount of effort which they spent not really doing very much else.

Family Dollar had been running into trouble for some time: between 2010 and 2013 they had opened an incredible 1,500 new stores, but unfortunately the cost of these (and often poor choice of locations which meant that they had started to cannibalise sales from their own stores) had reduced margins considerably and debt had doubled over the same period to $500 million.[146] Conversely, up until that point, Dollar Tree had remained profitable by sticking to its core principles (everything *was* $1 or less), but now felt it needed to move into the 'calls-itself-a-dollar-store-but-isn't' market, which was being dominated by Dollar General and Family Dollar, who had long abandoned this pretence as they increasingly went head-to-head (selling discounted merchandise at *any* price) with Walmart. With its new acquisition, Dollar Tree needed to move quickly to both integrate and therefore prove the logic of the deal, and also to stop the haemorrhaging of sales as the takeover battle had started to dominate proceedings. In the last quarter of 2015, earnings per share fell 13%, even though sales were up with the addition of the new-business volumes.

In the UK, Poundland's acquisition of rival 99p Stores was also referred to the UK equivalent of the FTC, the Competition and Markets Authority (CMA), which cleared the deal in August 2015. Blaming in part the extended regulatory review for the decline,[147] 12 months later the newly merged businesses reported sales down 3.9% and pre-tax profits down a whopping 84%. Faced with this, Poundland took the decision to rebrand all the old 99p Stores to Poundland, converting 235 stores and selling or closing 17 more; relegating what was no doubt initially intended as a strategic investment to simply an acquisition of more retail space in what was already a buyers' market. A deal that had already cost its shareholders an initial £55 million was followed by a share price collapse from 350p to 150p, and the subsequent sale of the business to Steinhoff

International, the German bargain-basement purchaser of bargain-basement businesses. In the financial year to March 2016, at time of writing the last one reported, the 99p Stores portfolio contributed a pre-tax hit of £9.8 million[148] to the bottom line.

For companies which it would be reasonable to assume would know each other's businesses so well, this is astonishing. It is as if the acquiring business is taken by surprise and dazed by the simple fact of its purchase, and temporarily forgets the rationale behind the deal in the first place. It becomes obsessed by small differences in operating model or style, under the illusion that maybe this is what made the acquired business tick, concealing some magic trick which must be discovered and preserved at all costs. In reality of course, it is the acquiring business which is, generally speaking, the most successful and experienced one and should be applying its own business principles as quickly as possible. Instead, the whole process gets dragged out, with often fatal consequences, exposing the fact that the rationale for buying the business in the first place was probably more opportunistic than strategic.

With the Granada UK operations, Compass Group suffered from no such hesitation. Here was a business model it thoroughly understood and, helped by considerable experience of successfully integrating large acquisitions previously, it was able to move quickly and decisively, and deliver significant benefits almost immediately. Much of this was undoubtedly helped by Compass Group, in common with some other service organisations and in contrast with other types of consumer businesses, having an inherently simple organisational model. Between the operational staff in the unit (which is where the majority of its 500,000 employees worldwide work) and the managerial staff who work in sales or administration, there is very little else. Apart from in the vending business, there is no operational infrastructure (and a correspondingly low utilisation of capital): food deliveries are performed almost exclusively by the suppliers; and other than a few offices, it has no premises or other assets. Although raw materials (i.e. food) constitute up to 50% of the cost base, it is a service company. It could be argued that (compared with a manufacturing or consumer products business, for example) it doesn't have too many complex processes to worry about, and therefore integration should be easy.

And this may be true, but those processes and the organisational structures which support them are still the lifeblood of a company, and getting them wrong, as another services outsourcing firm, Capita, found out recently, can have serious consequences.[149] Depending largely on its UK operations to deliver good results (unlike Compass Group which only relies on the UK for c.15% of its income[150]), Capita blamed post-Brexit uncertainty for its dismal 2016 results. The biggest loser in (and exiter from) the FTSE100 that year (its shares fell 50% to a 10-year low of £5.21, in a market which rose 14.4% to an all-time high during the same period), it had also faced a string of problems with changes to contracts which it had failed to deal with properly and which ultimately cost its CEO, Andy Parker, as well as a swathe of other senior managers, their jobs.[151]

Plus ça change, plus c'est la même chose

It might be thought that a major issue which would need careful handling is that acquiring a competitor could have serious ramifications in terms of client perception. After all, maybe not that long ago, the client involved had chosen the target company instead of you, probably after a heated battle where you were found to be (at best) number two. This is in practice less of an issue than might be imagined, for some of the reasons already stated above: the client is not buying a company, but a highly customised product and a similarly highly tailored contract to run it, and neither of those will change as a result of the change of ownership. There may be opportunities for renegotiation later, but for now, everything (apart from some minor signage maybe) will remain exactly the same. Whoever actually runs them, most staff canteens are branded by the company whose employees eat there, either to reflect in some way the identity of the business (at easyJet, for example, the original staff canteen was called the 'Orangery'), or to encourage an atmosphere of somehow having a break from work.[152] They are not usually identified as being run by, for example, Eurest or Sutcliffe Catering, except maybe in the very small print at the bottom of the menu. In addition, virtually every catering contract is unique in terms of location, layout, product and service offering, and of course price.[153] We shall look more closely in the next section at how companies should go about buying such services, and particularly the issue of creating contestable markets, but a foodservice contract is highly bespoke and so tightly specified that a client can be pretty confident that in practice nothing much will change. Of course, this is not true for the acquiring company, who, as we've discussed, will be planning to benefit from the increased purchasing power the new volumes bring, and can usually, even after sharing some of it with the new business's existing clients to sweeten the deal, rely on keeping the majority of the savings.

And maybe (if drawing conclusions rather than simply attempting to identify lessons is permissible in this instance) this is the most critical thing about managing change: that it is important to concentrate not only on what *is* changing, but what *isn't*; that while change is being affected in one part of an organisation, you also need to keep a very wary eye on the rest of the knitting to ensure it doesn't unravel somewhere else. After all, as we've seen constantly throughout these examples, the most intractable problems are caused not by the things which you might be explicitly doing to an organisation, but (following the Law of Unintended Consequences and mandated by System Dynamics) by their almost always unconsidered and therefore completely unanticipated side-effects.

Being employed throughout my career in roles where my major responsibility was to plan and deliver change, in one instance I believe I did the most good by preventing it. Joining an organisation on the cusp of a critical juncture in its history – that incredibly dangerous time when it has to stop being a small, 'start-up minded'[154] company and start laying the solid foundations for the next phase of its growth[155] – I picked up an IT department with the longest list of outstanding development requests that I'd ever seen. Although many of these were small, some were significant pieces of work; but the one thing which they all had in common was that they represented an amount of business change which individually might also have varied, but taken together (had they actually been delivered) would have brought the company to its knees. Seen as the bottleneck (and it was), the IT team had no way of prioritising, never mind actually delivering, what was on the list. Meetings to try and unblock the 'issues' with the developers (described variously and in no uncertain terms as inefficiency, obstructiveness or simply incompetence, and run by a CEO who saw the development department – all of whom had to attend – as his own personal fiefdom) were fractious and inconclusive. My first and most difficult job was to resolve this impasse, a task I accomplished by the incredibly simple but equally incredibly unpopular action of stopping everything. Every single one of the 'change requests' (which is what they were called, but which contained no indication of what that actually implied) was cancelled, and the function which had requested them (and which hadn't been present at any of the review meetings) was asked to resubmit them with two additional pieces of information: the actual business benefits (measured in hard cash) and a statement of how they were actually going to be delivered along with the impact of that on the rest of the organisation. Everyone concerned cried foul: their profit plans for this year were going to be badly hit if their particular project wasn't done immediately; what were the 'IT department' doing challenging their superior wisdom; and most telling, how on earth were they expected to produce this information?

Eventually common sense prevailed (after all, nothing

much appeared to have been delivered under the old method, even though in fact a great deal actually was, by a highly skilled but run-ragged group of developers), and the senior management team (now expanded beyond just the CEO) reluctantly agreed that this was a sensible way forward. Each of the department heads agreed to sponsor any initiative proposed by a member of their team, and priorities would be decided in strict business benefit order based on a rigorous set of value-for-money criteria. If they passed, they were on the list, and if there appeared to be more than one high-priority change at any one time (a difficult but critical judgement), and they were doable at the same time (in terms of both IT version control as well as business change management feasibility), they went ahead.

The most telling thing is that the size of the list, faced with clearing the dual hurdles of delivering real business benefit and also achievability, fell from more than a hundred requests to less than ten, and the IT team (whose output didn't really change very much other than for a slight increase because they didn't have to attend so many time-wasting meetings) started to be seen not as a bottleneck, but as adding real value.

Lesson 3: Simplicity is a strategy

Inevitably, any discussion of simplicity brings us back to easyJet. Very few other businesses have been built so rigorously on this principle, and have been able to stick so steadfastly to it as they have grown. There are many legends which survive from the early days of easyJet, and the constant retelling of them is one of the things which has preserved and disseminated to new employees the 'orange' culture as the company has grown. Passionate about being paperless from the very beginning (and that word is often misunderstood: it does not mean not using paper, it means not *storing* anything on paper, a very different thing), easyJet founder Stelios Haji-Ioannou was rumoured to go round the open-plan office after work each day with a bin liner, and sweep into it any paper which he found on *anyone's* desk, including the Chief Executive's. Whether it was true or not was irrelevant: it was a good story and served to make a powerful point.[156]

This approach brings together two inter-connected ideas: that of continual simplification, and that of avoiding complexity in the first place, and it is important to understand the differences. As we have seen previously, incremental complexity can sink a business, and in the case study in the previous chapter, the uncontrolled growth of systems, processes and organisational fragmentation had caused Dixons considerable difficulties. In *Simplicity-Minded Management,* Ron Ashkenas attributes growing (and out of control) complexity to four key issues: process evolution, managerial habits, product proliferation and what he calls structural mitosis.[157] It takes a very focussed company not to fall into at least one of those traps, and, as he describes, simply introducing large-scale, supposedly integrated, enterprise systems, without at the same time addressing the organisational issues and work behaviours, can often make things significantly worse.

Perhaps the most important managerial habit which seems to have been lacking in many of the examples discussed is the engineering mindset which can be summarised as 'only an engineer can *just* build a bridge'. We've come across this idea before in the Design to Cost department at Airbus, where before any part is put into final production, it is ruthlessly scrutinised for every opportunity to make it cheaper. In business, the equivalent would be a culture (rather than a separate department) which encouraged everyone in the organisation to spend a large percentage of their time thinking not 'what else could we do?', but 'what could we stop doing?'. There is no better illustration of this ethos than a story from the early days of the Japanese involvement in the US automotive industry, when in 1984 Toyota and General Motors entered into a joint venture at the Nummi (New United Motor Manufacturing Incorporated) plant in California, and the history of this somewhat controversial experiment (GM had gone into it hoping to learn the secrets of Japanese efficiency which was starting to badly hurt them in their home market, but in reality Toyota may have come away from it learning how to compete in the USA even better) has been well documented.[158] At one early meeting in Japan where GM staff had gone to start the learning process, one manager asked where the Quality Control department was situated. Their Japanese host, looking puzzled, asked what they meant, and when it was explained that in the US every company has a department which is responsible for quality, replied: '*So, if you have a separate department responsible for quality, what does everyone else do?*'[159]

The 'best of both worlds' myth

Compromise has been described as 'an intelligent answer to a complex question'. But this approach does not lead to simplicity, which is about eliminating things, not keeping them. And it is vitally important to think about, in trying to extract this 'best of both worlds' value, where this value really lies and what exactly it is that you want to keep.

In *Executing Your Business Transformation,*[160] Mark Morgan characterises the merger of AOL and Time Warner, if you could take the best of both worlds (for example, the product of one company and the organisation of the other), as a marriage made in heaven.[161] In reality, as he pithily points out, it was 'somewhere between mediocre and terrible', and was later described by Fortune magazine as 'the worst merger of all time'.[162] It is also an excellent example of a traditional company (Time Warner, which had conspicuously failed to develop an effective online presence) thinking it could make that magical leap (much as Dixons had done with Pixmania) into the new digital age through acquisition. What Time Warner had failed to spot, however, was that what it had thought of as the crown jewel of the merger – AOL's dial-up subscription service – was about to be completely destroyed by the new world of unmetered broadband. In trying to take the best of both worlds from the merger, what they actually did was take the worst, and in the process achieved the distinction of having to report in 2002 the largest annual loss in American corporate history of *$99 billion* (that's 99,000,000,000 US dollars, in case you didn't quite manage to take it in the first time),[163] a record which still stands today. The subsequent share price collapse wiped $206 billion off its valuation, an even more eye-watering amount.

What Compass Group was able to discover for itself (and this is an excellent example of what – as we haven't mentioned them for a while – management consultants call 'organisational learning'),[164] is that having common solutions, while appearing to offer simplicity and therefore lower cost, if they are deployed at the wrong point in the organisation, can in fact lead to just the opposite: greater complexity and higher cost. Very few businesses in reality need, never mind can justify, to run their entire worldwide operations on a single set of totally integrated processes. One obvious example is airlines, which need to have one single view of their inventory (seats) and of their operations (flights), and commonalty of information at the point where its front-of-house systems (which deal with passengers) meet its back-of-house systems (which concern planes and their crew). Anything less, and any fragility in these integrated systems is, as more than one airline has found to its cost recently, a recipe for disaster.

Standardisation therefore is not the same as simplification and can even be its direct opposite. Simplification is a mindset which says that at every stage of a process, in every part of a business, it should always be striving to do the minimum, with the least effort, and with the fewest resources. Having two systems, when one can do the job, is a prize worth fighting for, even if the cost of that in the short term may appear to outweigh any immediate return.

Cheapest *is* best

When organisations buy things which are not for resale (for example everything from, as this is about Compass Group, catering to IT systems; 'non-merchandise purchasing' as such things are called in retail parlance), or are not a main component of their business (as, for example, are aircraft for an airline), it is amazing how often they seem to forget the basic principle which underpins all purchasing decisions, which is: spend as little money as possible.

Readers may already be bridling at such a statement: *But won't that result in a shoddy or substandard product? What about quality? What about functionality? You do get what you pay for, of course.*

Unfortunately, all these miss the fundamental point, which is about the purchasing process, and that consists of two, very distinct stages: Stage 1 – decide exactly what the product must do, based on what you need; and Stage 2 – identify all the products that fulfil those criteria; and then, and only then, buy the cheapest. After all, why would you then pay more, because you're not going to get anything useful for the extra money? Taking into account that other thorny topic which we've touched on before – Total Cost of Ownership (TCO) – which says you need to consider not just the initial price you pay, but also the price you will continue to pay as long as you own it, you really do want to buy the cheapest.

The issue is cheapest of what? And the answer is the cheapest of all those products which are Fit for Purpose. Here, the difficulty is two-fold: firstly, it is precisely defining what Fit for Purpose actually means; and secondly, it is rigorously sticking to the discipline of a two-stage process. It is surprising how often this core point is ignored or conveniently forgotten, resulting in a spiral of confused thinking which can be summarised by the following two, actually completely unrelated, statements: This one is cheaper, but this one is better.

What is Fit for Purpose?

The first stage of the process is to define as clearly as possible what the *minimum* requirement is for the new system. The reason for this is not to then be able to say (as many people then do) that Solution A is better because it has more than the minimum, but because *the minimum is all you need*.

This cannot be stated strongly enough. The minimum, provided it genuinely includes everything which is needed to make the system work and deliver the benefits, is also the maximum. If you are going to build an aeroplane, why use a thicker or stronger material for the wings if a thinner or weaker one (and isn't that an emotionally loaded word in this context?) is strong enough? Indeed, if the cost of purchasing the stronger material is higher, or the thicker material is heavier, to make this decision would be folly, as there would be a forever ongoing cost of ownership (that TCO again) in the extra fuel needed to fly it around (remember, for no benefit). In engineering, this is so blindingly obvious that it is a core part of every design which is to be manufactured; it is the evaluation of the cost-benefit of every decision about

186

every component. Indeed, in the most complex engineering designs, for example (as we have discussed previously) at Airbus, the Design To Cost department will re-evaluate every previous engineering decision to see whether it is optimal in terms of being the cheapest solution which is still Fit for Purpose. Indeed, with the latest A380s selling for a shade under $430 million each (2015 list price, discounts negotiable for volume orders), and with a development cost of over $25 billion to amortise, ensuring every part of the airframe and manufacturing process conforms to this principle is the only way they can make any money.[165]

This is a fine art – the intention is not to produce a wing which is so light and weak that it fails: the intention is to produce one which is light and weak enough that (given the safety tolerances of stress, maintenance and lifetime usage, all of which are integral parts of the Fit for Purpose definition) it *just* doesn't. Why should this be any different for computer systems?

The water is often muddied the most by the vendors of software and services themselves, who of course have the most to lose by purchasers buying the cheapest solutions. They will be the first to talk-up the superior features of their products (without explaining, even if asked, superior to what); aiming to convince often infrequent buyers that quality is the over-riding consideration. And of course it is a critical issue, but only as far as the product in question does or doesn't meet the minimum quality standard defined in the Fit for Purpose specification. If it meets the minimum, great, it's on the list; if it doesn't, it's not. It's as simple as that. How much it exceeds that minimum threshold, and the enthusiasm with which the sales force are pushing that aspect, should sound a very loud warning bell. The one thing you can be certain of is that this means extra cost, now and probably forever.

Don't listen either to the argument that the extra features will deliver extra benefits: firstly, you haven't identified those, and therefore have no way of delivering them (assuming you have for the benefits you *have* identified), and secondly, they probably won't; most features highlighted in sales presentations being optimised (as the not entirely cynical phrase goes) for use in a PowerPoint presentation rather than in the real world. Of course, having identified all the products which meet the criteria and then bought the cheapest, if the one you have chosen does have additional features which you can then exploit at some later time, so much the better, as long as that didn't figure in any way in the purchasing decision.

Creating that minimum definition, apart from the discipline required, comes with other challenges, namely the need to consider not just current requirements, but future ones, and to include financial parameters without getting side-tracked into purchase cost, which is not a feature of the process until Stage 2. It is perfectly acceptable for the creation of the definition to be an iterative process, exploring different products to learn about the market and the art of the possible, and conducting trials to see what might work. It is vital, though, that it is always clear that this is only part of this first stage, not part of the decision-making, and being true to this is often difficult. The definition of course can, and indeed ought to include elements of cost: it might state, for example, that the ongoing maintenance cost should not be more than, say, 5% of the original purchase price, or that the solution should be implementable within a certain timeframe (implying cost as well as achievability). The greatest part of the definition will be about function, however, and this is where the hardest work lies. As well as hard metrics, function points and maybe some cost elements, the definition should also include (and these may be some of the most important considerations) soft criteria: is the management philosophy of the supplier aligned with ours? How willing are they to commit to a long-term strategic partnership to develop their business as well as ours? What is their relative size (both in terms of long term viability, and also importance to each other of the relationship)?

Once the final specification is produced, that is the time to hold it up to the light and see what, if anything, fits. It may well be, of course, that once the Fit for Purpose definition is published (perhaps in the form of a Request for Proposals (RFP) or a formal Tender) only one, maybe two, or worst case, NO products can match it. If that is the case, it will be very difficult, or indeed impossible to progress to the next stage – price – as for that to be effectively negotiated, a contestable market needs to exist. There is no point being a buyer in a sellers' market: suppliers need to want to do business with you, and in order to win the order, they need to know that they must offer the lowest price. This is not the time for compromise, however; this is the time to start getting creative.

Meanwhile, back at easyJet

Along with the other key factors mentioned in an earlier chapter, it has always been accepted wisdom that having a single manufacturer's fleet is an essential ingredient of low-cost airline operations, and at the outset, easyJet was 100% Boeing. It is now 100% Airbus, but for a while between 2002 and 2011 it *did* operate a mixed fleet, and the story of how and why this came about is an excellent case study in creating a contestable market to drive purchasing power.

The Boeing 737 had become the reference aircraft for those seeking to start up in the airline industry; most famously Southwest Airlines, established in 1971, who had started operations from Love Field in downtown Dallas. The 737 is, even today, still largely a mechanical aircraft; easy to operate and with predictable costs. They are also in plentiful supply and so not hard to get hold of. The Airbus A320, by contrast, is a very sophisticated, software-driven machine, which in the early 2000s was still establishing itself in the market, and certainly had not got any traction in the emerging low-cost airline market. Then 9/11 struck and nobody in the world was buying aircraft; except that is for a couple of low-cost airlines in Europe, Ryanair and easyJet, both of whom had emerged following the deregulation of the market and implementation in 2000 of the Single European Sky initiative.[166]

easyJet recognised in Airbus' ambition a huge opportunity – Ryanair had just ordered 100 more 737s (plus the option of 50 more) and the big question was whether easyJet would follow suit. Airbus had other ideas and saw this as *their* opportunity to establish themselves into this new market. Ironically, Go Fly was also looking to purchase aircraft in early 2002, to carry forward their ambitious expansion plans under new owners 3i, but unbeknown to the Go management team, 3i had other ideas, and as majority shareholder, had already agreed to sell out to easyJet. This only strengthened easyJet's negotiating hand, and by combining both airlines' needs, they were able to place with Airbus the then largest order for single-aisle aircraft in Europe (120 aircraft plus an option for another 120).[167]

During the transition period from Boeing, Airbus guaranteed easyJet a lower cost of ownership than they had previously enjoyed in terms of service costs and staff cross-training (a big issue, as is crew rostering with a mixed fleet), plus they gave easyJet a great price for the purchase (rumoured to be a 60% discount) in order to win a long-term deal which was strategically important to them. The first of these was enough to meet one of the most important criteria in easyJet's strategy: that buying Airbus would not lead to higher operating costs, and the now highly contested market led to the second, the lowest possible price.

As Ray Webster, easyJet's CEO at the time of the initial deal, said, '*our long-term aim is that Boeing and Airbus will be interchangeable. We wanted to make sure we didn't believe our own public relations too much*'.[168] By 'interchangeable', Webster of course meant 'can be played off against each other indefinitely'; he did not mean easyJet would have a long-term mixed-fleet strategy.

A similar example in a different field of purchasing

also concerns easyJet. For companies basing their entire business and therefore future survival on the effective use of technology (as easyJet had done almost from the very beginning with their reservation systems and easyJet.com), systems availability, especially in the new internet world, is a critical issue. In this environment, the discussion rapidly moves on from what used to be known as Disaster Recovery (DR) to 100% availability, no matter what. When more than 98% of your income[169] and 100% of your operational capability depends on your systems being up, it stops being a question of how quickly you can restore them if they fail, but becomes a question of how to prevent them going down in the first place. This is another issue which the traditional airlines, with their myriad of antiquated systems, have found it very hard to address, as British Airways recently found more than once to their cost.[170] easyJet, much as they had done with Boeing and Airbus, was able to create a contestable market where before none had existed by tendering for an outsourced IT hosting supplier who could offer a guarantee of 100% uptime, with penalties of 100% of the hosting fees for any failure. Their Fit for Purpose specification also included a guarantee from the chosen supplier that for each year of the contract, the cost would be a fixed percentage lower than the previous period on a per-passenger-seat-flown basis.[171] Eight companies attended the open-house briefing session to discuss the tender at easyLand, at which several of the (again, traditionally minded) suppliers, including IBM and BT, were extremely dismissive of the proposal and stated loudly that it was not possible and we were wasting everyone's time. Two companies, however, and two is enough, saw this as a major and possibly unique opportunity, given the timing, to launch their new business offerings in the emerging 'high-availability' market, which they (quite rightly as it happens) predicted would rapidly become the norm. easyJet was a customer they had to win. The subsequent battle to secure this critical contract (which didn't involve easyJet backing down on a single one of its supposedly impossible demands) led to the lowest possible price for the highest possible service, and a relationship with the successful bidder, Savvis, which is still in place more than 10 years later[172].

…and even further back at The Burton Group

A very similar example comes from my time at The Burton Group, one of the largest users in the UK and possibly Europe of what is known in the business as 'IBM mid-range technology'. This IT platform was a much lower-priced (although, being IBM and highly proprietary, still expensive) alternative to the traditional mainframes which many high-transaction-volume companies used at the time. It was a huge market;[173] up until the early 1990s dominated by IBM. The technology landscape was changing, however, and in an attempt to appear more 'open' (an over-used and much-misunderstood word in IT circles) and at the same time reduce its costs by commoditising some of the external components, they unwittingly opened the door to a group of previously little-regarded competitors. One of these was EMC, up until then a small player in the world of data storage. Desperate to gain a foothold in the lucrative and very large mid-range business, they were the perfect supplier to bid against IBM when The Burton Group went to market for a tripling of its data storage capacity in 1992. The motivation for this was partly business growth (and IFPR data needs contributed in no small measure to this, as we have discussed earlier), but mainly an increased need for resilience. With every part of the business now depending on IT one way or another, being able to rely on those systems being available was becoming more and more important. Increasing the disk storage enabled the IT team to implement a technique called 'mirroring', basically ensuring that the data was in two places at once in case one of the data storage arrays failed.

It was a huge order, and I can now reveal (the 25 years which was the non-disclosure period of this highly commercially sensitive deal having now passed), that EMC *gave the disks* to The Burton Group for nothing.[174] This was obviously a great deal for Burtons, but also for EMC, providing them with a springboard to grow into the world's largest supplier of high-availability disk storage equipment, eclipsing even IBM. Its revenues grew from a mere $120 million to $9 billion over the next 10 years, and enabled it to acquire the once-mighty Data General for $1.1 billion in 2002, purely for its disk technology.[175]

And what happened to Compass Group?

Despite an untypical, but not insignificant blip in 2004–2005 when the perhaps too operationally focussed board temporarily took their eye off the ball and allowed the exercise of strategic control to slip,[176] Compass Group has continued to grow and prosper. Always relying on its core principles of how to manage growth, it is now worth £25 billion, and is consistently one of the most valuable 30 companies in the UK FTSE100.

Coming out of the complex Granada deal, its name, logo, operating model and ethos remain unchanged. It still relies on the same back-office systems which were installed in the four years leading up to 2000, and its profit, earnings per share and dividend continue to rise each year, quietly delivering increasing returns to its investors. Between 1990 and 2000 it was the best-performing stock in terms of overall investor returns *in Europe,*[177] and between 2006 and 2017, it returned over £9 billion to investors through the main dividend, share buy-backs and special dividends. In 2014, Richard Cousins,[178] who succeeded Mike Bailey as Chief Executive in 2006, was ranked 65th in the Harvard Business Review's Top 100 CEOs in the world by shareholder returns, and had been promoted to 17th by 2016.[179]

It wins new contracts and opens new units on a daily basis, and occasionally still makes the odd 'in-fill' acquisition. The days of major transactions, however, appear to be over: maybe there just aren't any more big deals to be done, certainly not of the scale and complexity of the Granada one. Or maybe the company, having spent so much time, effort and thought on working out how to grow quickly, has now achieved cruising altitude and a more 'organic' growth rate.

It is still probably the largest company you've never heard of.

THE FINAL CUT

From the examples in this book it would be tempting to conclude that business change almost always goes wrong and that rapid growth in particular always poses serious and occasionally fatal challenges; and there do seem to be many more examples of failure than success. Maybe that is because on the one hand they make better stories, but on the other hand, who tells stories of successful outcomes except those responsible for them? And then who believes them?

The other question is whether there is more to be learnt from failure or success. Apparently we should learn from our failures otherwise we are destined to repeat them, and there must be much to learn, but on the other hand, human nature makes this the hardest thing to do: '*Yes, I got it wrong, but I'm not stupid, so why should I do that again? Let's just move on.*' Surely there is also a strong case to be made that the lessons which can be learnt from our successes are actually the most useful ones, because *those* are the ones we need to learn to repeat.

It is undoubtedly true that managing change is hard. And the hardest part is recognising it is happening in the first place, even if it is you who has initiated it. As we have seen, systems in the widest sense of the word are very powerful and often misunderstood. They are often confused with IT, and with a history of IT managers often having come up through the ranks as over-promoted programmers, this confusion is often not resolved. Business leaders rarely understand IT, and, as a rapidly evolving and highly mobile profession, it is often the case that IT managers do not fully understand the businesses in which they work, at least not in the early days of a new job, which is when they are under the most pressure to make a difference.

As we've also seen though, relatively speaking, IT systems are the easy ones to deal with; at least you know they're coming. It's the other kinds of systems which cause the problems. Any organisational change, any process change, however small, is a systems change. A new incentive scheme is one of the most powerful of these, acting directly on that most unpredictable element in every organisation, human beings, and it is therefore the one with the greatest potential to create the most uncertain outcomes. As the study of economics has come to embrace, change happens because people tend to act in their own best interests, and unless the results of those actions are anticipated and planned for, then the effects of them on the organisations in which they work can be profound and often undesirable.

When an organisation divides itself into internal divisions set up to do business with each other and their leaders are incentivised to maximise internal results, why should it be a surprise when that is exactly what the individuals concerned do? When a Chief Executive is incentivised to get the company's share price to £2, why is anyone taken by surprise when that is exactly what happens? When consultants are brought in to examine a highly centralised organisation, is it really a surprise when they recommend de-centralisation (and vice versa)?

The fact that these outcomes might be wholly contrary to the interests of the company's other key stakeholders, its customers and shareholders, and that the effects will have a huge negative impact on both, should really have been considered before they were implemented, not agonised over later in the post mortem.

What is most surprising is that none of the lessons we've looked at in these stories were particularly unique to the organisations concerned. For each one which I learned from direct experience, once I looked around, many more examples of exactly the same thing emerged. The only conclusion which can be drawn is that, rather like the moth to the proverbial candle, people tasked with making change are attracted by the brightest ideas – the most fashionable and exciting, rather than the prosaic but proven – and it is these former ones which frequently turn out to be the most dangerous, and most often lead to their downfall.

In summary, it must always be remembered that all businesses are, at a fundamental level, complex collections of systems – some logical and well-designed, many illogical and accidental – which make up the whole organisation. Understanding how these work individually is extremely hard, never mind together; and making sense of them, and deciding how to change them, is often simply a matter of good fortune. As Poul Anderson said:

'I have yet to see any problem, however complicated, which, when you looked at it in the right way, did not become still more complicated.'[180]

If there is one overall lesson which can be drawn from all the examples discussed here, it is that organisations are highly sensitive organisms which do not react well to invasive surgery. Meddle with them without taking the utmost care, and history shows us that there is a real danger that you will kill the patient – or, at the very least, fatally wound it.

Hopefully the stories related in this book will give reason to pause and think twice before picking up the scalpel.

NOTES

ENDNOTES

Introduction

1   *The E-Myth: Why Most Businesses Don't Work and What to Do About It,* Michael E Gerber, Ballinger Publishing, 1986.
2   *Winning,* Jack Welch, HarperTorch, 2005.
3   Good choice!

LA Story

4   Nowadays, Apple is probably the best known proponent of 'vertical integration', where a company owns and operates every aspect of its supply chain. For Apple, that means manufacturing its own chips, touch ID sensors and LCD screens; assembling the phones in factories it owns; and selling them through its own shops. For more information, see *When and When Not to Vertically Integrate*, J Stuckey

and D White, McKinsey Quarterly, No. 3, 1993, or *Vertical Integration, Outsourcing and Corporate Strategy*, KR Harrigan, Beard Books, 2003.

5   *Perspectives on Strategy: From the Boston Consulting Group*, Carl W Stern and George Stalk Jr (Eds), BCG 1998.

6   'Profit and Loss' accounts: along with a Balance Sheet, the periodic Financial statement of a business's performance. Published externally, as a minimum annually, their format and contents are highly regulated. Internally, a business normally produces monthly Management Accounts, which are basically tracks of performance against plan. An internal function producing a P&L usually indicates an organisation which has completely lost its way. Unconstrained by any generally accepted rules, they are anyway usually an exercise in the most creative of accounting practices.

7   Jim Maxmin later wrote a very interesting book with his wife that in part draws on his experiences at Laura Ashley: *The Support Economy: Why Corporations are Failing Individuals and the Next Episode of Capitalism*, Shoshana Zuboff and James Maxmin, Penguin, 2004. Incidentally, Jim Maxmin left with a payoff of £1.8 million in a year when the total profit was only £3 million, so the corporation certainly didn't fail *him*.

8   Alphonse Schouten was, interestingly, the European MD who had done such a good purchasing deal for the Manufacturing Division's cotton prints in 1988.

9   Blakeway Webb made £8 million on departure by selling 4 million shares back to the Ashley family, under a private agreement.

10 Bernard Ashley was heard to say he'd brought Ann Iverson in because 'we need a woman at the helm, like the good old

days'. A senior manager, amongst others from that time, said that this was felt to be a 'fairly offensive period', with 'an unpleasant way of working'.

11 Quoted in *Ashley's Road to Robertson*, Julia Finch, The Guardian, 22/01/1999, which attempts to explain the bizarre appointment.

12 If a temporary share rise at the bottom of the cycle is referred to as a 'dead cat bounce', the behaviour of LA's shares at the top might similarly be described as a 'dead seagull thermal'.

13 *The Financial Aspects of Corporate Governance (The 'Cadbury Report')*, Gee, 1992.

14 In the 1990s, LA's share ownership was c.60% MUI and Chairman Tan Sri Dr Khoo Kay Peng's investment vehicle, and 24% Ashley family, leaving in effect only 16% publically and regularly traded. The Ashley family sold their last remaining shares in 2001.

15 *The Management Myth: Management Consulting Past, Present and Largely Bogus*, by Matthew Stewart, Norton, 2009, has many revealing insights into the business of management consultancy.

16 *Management Consulting: Delivering an Effective Project*, Philip A Wickham, Pearson, 1999.

17 *The Goal: A process of ongoing improvement*, Eliyahu M Goldratt, Jeff Cox, North River Press, 1984.

18 *Who says elephants can't dance?* Louis Gerstner, Harper Collins, NY, 2002.

19 *Duran's Quality Control Handbook*, Joseph M Juran, McGraw-Hill, 1951.

20 Quoted in *Classic Drucker*, Harvard Business Review Books, 2006.

21 Those wonderful pre-digital strips of images printed directly from the negatives without any enlargement.

22 *Contemporary Strategy Analysis*, Robert M Grant, Wiley, 2004.

23 Cited in *Project Management: A Systems Approach to Planning, Scheduling, and Controlling*, Harold Kerzner, John Wiley & Sons, 2006.

24 The modern term for a phenomenon first discussed by Adam Smith in *The Wealth of Nations*, published in 1776.

25 *Theory of the firm: Managerial behaviour, agency costs and ownership structure.* Jensen, Michael C and William H Meckling, 1976. Journal of Financial Economics (October), 3(4): 305–360.

26 *What Money Can't Buy,* Michael J Sandel, Farrar, Straus and Giroux, 2012. This book contains many fascinating examples of incentive schemes outside of the normal world of corporate remuneration and what results they can lead to.

27 *The Economic Approach to Human Behaviour,* Gary Becker, University of Chicago, 1976.

28 *Freakonomics: A Rogue Economist Explores the Hidden Side of Everything,* Steven D Levitt and Stephen J Dubner, New York: William Morrow, 2006.

29 The Beer Game – *Industrial Dynamics*, Jay Wright Forrester, MIT Press, 1961.

30 Although these lead times are made a mockery of nowadays by retailers such as Zara, (who even in the difficult world of fashion retail, often have total design to sales leadtimes of as little as two weeks, and are sampling and reacting to rates of sale at a store level on an hourly basis), they are by no means unusual. In the days of the retail case studies described here, lead times were usually calculated in months, and once plans

had been 'locked and loaded', it was the retailer who took all the risk of the ranges not selling.

31 *Encyclopaedia of play in today's society*, Rodney Carlisle, Sage, 2009.

Gone for a Burton

32 *The Burton Group Family Tree*, Charlotte Hardie, Retail Week, 11/09/2011.

33 These at the time included the chains Burton Menswear, Dorothy Perkins, Evans, IS, Topshop, Topman, Principles for Women, Principles for Men and Champion Sport.

34 Including the most creative management accountant I've ever worked with, who taught me everything I might have wanted to know (and much, including for legal reasons, that I didn't) about 'bunce' and 'teeming and lading', as he called it.

35 It is a little-known fact that people in Scotland, for example, tend to be shorter and wider than their compatriots south of the border.

36 *A Practical Approach to Merchandising Mathematics*, Linda M Cushman, Bloomsbury Publishing Plc, 2015, is a good introduction to the complexities of merchandise planning.

37 There is a great story of a group of City traders who were known to outperform their colleagues every year, and that their success lay in a spreadsheet model which they had created and maintained in great secrecy. One day they all resigned to go and join a rival firm and panic ensued. It was vital to get hold of the magic spreadsheet before they took it and it was lost to their current firm. However it was done, the model

was secured, but on examination was found to be full of the simplest of errors, plusses and minuses the wrong way round and the like. The reality was that, although all their decisions had been based on its output, it would have performed no better than a random number generator.

38 This was conveniently just before the Trade Union and Labour Relations (Consolidation) Act 1992 came into force in June of that year, requiring consultation for large-scale lay-offs.

39 Although when I joined, in 1991, it was still traditional for new directors to have a suit made to measure for them. There remained one stalwart from the old days, an elderly gentleman whom I visited in the hidden depths of the Leeds warehouse in order to be measured up. Feeling pleased with myself and wanting to show that, even as a relative youngster, I knew how this worked, I asked when the fitting was. *'What do you think we are, a f*@#ing tailors?'* he replied with scorn in a strong Yorkshire accent, putting me firmly in my place.

40 A classic example, for the financial nerds, is the representation of 'profit' versus 'earnings', as stated in the two hotly debated (in financial nerdery circles) terms of PBIT (Profit before Interest and Tax) and EBITDA (Earnings before Interest Tax, Depreciation and Amortisation). The first is often given (especially in the company's own statements) as the true performance of a business; savvy commentators know to ignore this, and look at EBITDA, as this excludes the two most fudgable items in the accounts, the depreciation of tangible assets (over how many years? Are they really assets? Where are they now? etc) and the amortisation of intangibles. I particularly love the idea of accounting for 'intangibles'; these are often things such as brand value, or goodwill, and

can be basically any number you care to think of. If anyone is interested in learning more about this, *Creative Accounting, Fraud and International Accounting Scandals* by MJ Jones, Wiley, 2010, is a ripping read.

41 *Logistics and Retail Management: Emerging Issues and New Challenges in the Retail Supply Chain*, John Fernie, Kogan Page, 2009.

42 A simple example, which I had to deal with, was systems: do you use the Burton systems for their shops in Debenhams, thus keeping intact the integrity of their back-office infrastructure, or use the Debenhams ones (which were of course different), thus making it easier to manage the physical stores? Much argued about, this was never satisfactorily resolved.

43 *Strategic Management: Awareness & Change*, John L Thompson, Frank Martin, Cengage Learning, 2010, has the story.

44 Daryl R Connor is often credited with first using this phrase in his book *Managing at the Speed of Change*, Random House, 1992.

45 *The Millennium Bug: How to Survive it: How to Survive the Coming Chao*s, MS Hyatt, Regnery Publishing Inc, 1998, is as good as any source at portraying the looming apocalypse, and stories like this were highly influential at the time in persuading companies and their shareholders to take the issue seriously.

46 In 2017, one well-known high street name is known to be still running an element of its portfolio on MS-DOS.

47 These costs, however, are frequently ignored, or as a minimum, grossly underestimated. The costs (and some of the reasons for this omission) could easily be the subject for a whole book,

and indeed have been so many times. *Enterprise Software TCO: Calculating and Using Total Cost of Ownership for Decision Making*, S Snapp, SCM Focus, 2013, is one such example.

48 *Garment Tag Equipment*, OG Hessler, Proceedings of the Review of Input and Output Equipment Used in Computer Systems, American Institute of Electrical Engineers Computer Conference, 1952.

49 *17 Billion Reasons to Say Thanks: The 25th Anniversary of the U.P.C. and Its Impact on the Grocery Industry*, Price Waterhouse Coopers, 1999.

50 *The Information Paradox*, Fujitsu Consulting with John Thorp, United Features, 1996.

51 *The Motivation to Work*, F Herzberg, B Mausner, and B B Snyderman, Wiley, 1959.

52 *Implementing Information for Health: Even More Challenging than Expected?*, Professor Denis Protti, London: Department of Health, 2002.

53 Operations Management: A Strategic Approach, Ed. A Bettley, D Mayle and T Tantoush, Open University, 2005, and *IT-Enabled Business Transformation: From Automation to Business Scope Redefinition*, N Venkatraman, MIT Sloan Management Review, Winter 1994.

54 *What Really Works: The 4+2 Formula for Sustained Business Success*, William Joyce, Nitin Nohria and Bruce Roberson, Harper Business, 2011.

I remember stopping a failing project at The Burton Group shortly after joining. After a short review, it was clear it could have become a case study in how to spot change: the project manager had left the company a few months earlier and not been replaced, and the project sponsor *had died*. Sad, but impossible not to be impressed by the single-mindedness of a project team who hadn't considered either of these facts to be material.

55 *The Mythical Man-Month: Essays on Software Engineering*, Fred Brooks, Addison-Wesley, 1975.

56 For some projects, building x miles of road, for example, scope is much easier to define than for others. History is full, however, of stories of these kinds of projects running late and/or over someone's budget. Not all of them can be attributed to an unexpected discovery of Roman remains, so the assumption has to be that the nature of the problem wasn't fully understood ('scoped') at the outset.

57 *Managing Successful Projects with Prince 2*, Office of Government Commerce, The Stationary Office, 2009.

58 *Extreme Programming Explained: Embrace Change*, K Beck, Addison Wesley, 1999.

59 *Why Good Projects Fail Anyway*, Nadim F Matta and Ronald N Ashkenas, Harvard Business Review, September 2003.

60 *The CHAOS Report*, Standish Group, 2016.

61 *Titanic Lessons for IT Projects*, M Kozak-Holland, Multimedia Publications, 2004.

62 *Broken Promises? FoxMeyer's Project was a Disaster. Was the Company Too Aggressive or was it Misled?* J Jesitus, Industry Week, 03/11/1997.

63 *History in the Making*, D Corsten, ECR Journal Vol 5, No.1, Summer 2005. See also '*Transforming the Supply Chain*', D Corsten and R Slagmunder, INSEAD, 2003.

64 *The Dismantled National Programme for IT in the NHS*, House of Commons Public Accounts Committee report, 18/09/2013.

65 *The Coming Commoditization of Processes*, TH Davenport, Harvard Business Review, June 2005.

66 It is important to understand that in business there are two kinds of costs: costs I have control over which are, by definition, fine; and costs I have no control over, which are, by definition, too high.

67 *To Centralise or Not to Centralise?* A Campbell, S Kunisch and G Muller-Stewens, McKinsley Quarterly, June 2011.

68 *Die Another Day: What Leaders Can Do About the Shrinking Life Expectancy of Corporations*, M Reeves and L Peuschel, bcg. perspectives, Boston Consulting Group, 02/07/2015.

69 *Review of Major Companies Merger Failures in The First Decade of 21st Century*, R Shukla, International Journal of Enhanced Research in Management & Computer Applications, March 2014.

70 Office 2013 licenses can now be transferred to another PC, Lance Whitney, c.net, 06/03/2013. The reason why Microsoft were doing this was to try to push users onto the initially cheaper, but in the long run much more profitable, online subscription service, Office 365.

71 *The 10 Worst Product Fails of All Time*, Thomas C Frolich, Time Magazine, 06/03/2014.

72 The pension fund deficit was £993 million in April 2017, reported in The Guardian, 01/04/2017.

73 *Business Insider UK*, Oscar Williams-Grut, 08/05/2016.

74 It is impossible not to admire the sheer financial bravado of all this: when he bought Arcadia in 2002, Green only put in £10 million of his own cash. As he is quoted as saying, "Arcadia is probably the single best investment anyone ever made from a £10m equity". Quoted in *Financial Time*s, 21/10/2005.

The French Connection

75 Although to be fair to the Managing Directors of the retail chains, whose minds were generally entirely focussed on hitting the numbers, this description is more applicable to some of the older-school directors in other areas. As part of my induction, I was pleased to meet Geoffrey Budd, a charming gentleman and Company Secretary for the last 35 years. I was offered a cup of tea in his nicely-appointed office; with the sound of willow on leather and the commentary murmuring gently in the background, he asked me how I was finding things in my first few weeks. '*Oh, you know how it is when you join a new company,*' I said noncommittally. '*No,*' he replied as he offered me a biscuit.

76 Freeserve was the first mass-market dial-up Internet Service Provider (ISP) in the UK. It made its money by offering 'free' internet access to subscribers, who used a local telephone number to connect. The innovation was that, although the internet access itself was free, the call (although cheap) wasn't, and Freeserve made over 50% margin from the cost of the dial-up. It was launched in 1998 and floated on the stock market in July 1999, at which point they had approximately 1.3 million subscribers (more than the incumbent telephone provider, BT) and was valued at nearly £1.5 billion. It was later bought by the French ISP Wanadoo for £1.65 billion, but struggled to make a profit in the increasingly unmetered broadband market. Dixons made over £650 million from their share.

77 Elkjörp made no secret of their 'upsell' business model: lead products were advertised heavily discounted, but only limited

numbers of those were actually available in the stores, and instead the sales assistants were heavily incentivised to sell higher-ticket-price and higher-margin products in their place.

78 The logic behind this was the belief that customers really wanted to view as well as buy products, and valued service. Whether this was entirely true or not was beside the point: Dixons had a large and expensive estate of high street and out-of-town stores, and needed to utilise them as much as they could. It was certainly true that customers liked browsing in shops before ordering; the problem had been that they were then going online to order the products from other retailers who were either cheaper or offered quicker delivery. In response to this, Dixons was one of the first to offer 'collect at store', a variation of the 'click and collect' approach, where a customer could order online and then pick up the product in store, often within the hour.

79 The attraction to the Rosenblums, apart from the cash, was access to Dixons' distribution network, especially in the UK, which would therefore allow them to start selling white goods and other large items which required delivery and maybe installation.

80 Dynamic packaging is most often seen in the travel industry, where flights, hotels and car hire, for example, can be bought as separate products within a single transaction, individually selected by the customer rather than sold as a pre-bundled package. For more details of how this works, see *Hospitality Information Systems and e-Commerce*, Dana V Tesone, John Wiley and Sons, New York, 2005. In Pixmania, this involved offering accessories such as batteries, cases and memory cards which could be selected during a camera sale, tailored both

to the customer needs, and more importantly, to maximising margins. As in travel dynamic packaging, the final price would then appear as an offer, disguising the individual prices and margins.

81 The story of Browett's controversial hiring (including an enormous 'golden hello' of £36 million in shares) and subsequent firing six short months later makes interesting further reading on how cultures can collide with catastrophic consequences. See, for example, *Why new Apple retail chief's British predecessor John Browett was fired*, J Titcomb, The Telegraph, London, 15/10/2012 et al.

82 The story of how this knowledge was transferred from the e-Merchant support staff in Paris to the Czech software engineers in the newly created extension to the off-shored support centre in Brno is yet another story of worlds colliding.

83 *Edge Strategy: A New Mindset for Profitable Growth*, Alan Lewis and Dan McKone, Harvard Business Review Press, January 2016.

84 *Microsoft Insider: Here's why we bought Skype*, Matt Rosoff, Business Insider, 12/05/2011

85 *Microsoft pays VirnetX $23 million to settle expanded patent case,* MJ Foley, for ZDNet, 19/12/2014.

86 *How Autonomy Fooled Hewlett-Packard*, JT Ciesielski, Fortune Magazine, 14/12/2016.

87 The European businesses including Elkjorp, Electro World, and Kotsovolos were acquired piecemeal between 1999 and 2005 and run as stand-alone operations.

88 *Mergers and Acquisitions Involving UK Companies*, Office of National Statistics (ONS) Bulletins, 2007–2017.

89 See numerous case studies on Marks and Spencer and Burger

King in France, J Sainsbury in Egypt, Tesco in the US et al.

90 In 1999, Carrefour and Promodes merged, supposedly as a defensive move in case Walmart came to call, but nothing transpired, despite them having initial talks with Auchun.

91 *Accor to acquire online home rental site Onefinestay*, M Ahmed and A Thomson, Financial Times, 05/04/2016.

92 *The knowledge-creating company: How Japanese companies create the dynamics of innovation*, I Nonaka and H Takeuchi, OUP, 1995.

93 *Advances in Computer and Information Sciences and Engineering*, T Sobh, Springer Netherlands, 2008.

94 *Artificial Intelligence: A New Synthesis*, NJ Nilsson, Morgan Kaufmann, 1998.

95 During the project, I was pleased to meet the young designer who was responsible for the handle on the toilet doors, and his enthusiasm and commitment (and the quality of the end product) were as impressive and genuine as that of the old hands doing the wings.

96 There is the now infamous incident in 1999 when NASA lost the $125 million Mars Observer because the sub-contractor Lockheed Martin's engineering team had used English units of measurement while the NASA team had used the metric system for calculating altitude. The subsequent enquiry concluded that the spacecraft was 100 kilometres (note: kilometres) too close to Mars when it tried to enter orbit around the planet and burned up. This problem is not new: one of the reasons given for why Christopher Columbus believed he had found the East Indies when he had sailed a mere 3,000 miles west from Cape St Vincent in Portugal was that he had done his own calculations to plot their

position, using information derived from calculations done by the Persian geographer Alfraganus in around 860AD. Unfortunately, he had assumed Alfraganus was using the Roman mile (4,856 feet) when in fact he was using the Arabic mile (7,091 feet), which, compounded with other erroneous assumptions, resulted in an error of nearly 6,000 miles.

97 The most famous example being Ronald Reagan's supposed statement: *'the trouble with the Russians is that they don't have a word for détente'*. Quoted in numerous sources.

98 A more straightforward example is *Business operations in France*, E Milhac, Bloomberg, 2016. A good example of an article which covers the softer aspects well is *French Business Culture and Etiquette*, E Breukel, published in InterCultural Communication, retrieved 02/06/2017.

99 A point about cultural differences was brought home forcibly during dinner one evening in Charlotte, NC, USA, when someone remarked that they would be sitting down at the same moment in Spain to eat the same meal; 'dinner' in the USA often being eaten at 5.30pm and in Spain at 11.30pm – the exact same moment given the 6-hour time difference.

100 *easyLand – How easyJet Conquered Europe*, Tony Anderson, Grosvenor House, 2014 is a good read, as is *easyJet: The story of Britain's Biggest Low-Cost Airline*, Lois Jones, Aurum Press, 2005, which covers the start up and early years.

101 See the CAA ruling on the matter, Applications 1B/423/1 and 1B/423/2 by Go Fly Limited heard on 8 November 1999, and *Superbrands case studies: easyJet*, first published in *Consumer Superbrands, Volume V*, March 2003.

102 *An Airline Adventure,* Barbara Cassani and Kenny Kemp, Sphere, 2005.

103 *DSG outsources to HCL: A Case Study*, OVUM Consulting, 2010

104 *The Change Game: How Today's Global Trends are Shaping Tomorrow's Companies*, Peter Lawrence, Kogan Page, 2002.

105 *Internet — Technical Development and Applications,* E Tkacz and A Kapczynski, Springer, 2009. The first pilot system was actually installed in Tesco in the UK and first demonstrated in 1979 by Michael Aldrich, although John Markoff suggests in his book *What the Dormouse Said: How the Sixties Counterculture Shaped the Personal Computer Industry*, (Penguin, 2005) that the first online e-commerce transaction may have been a drugs deal conducted in 1971 or 1972 between students at Stanford University's and Boston's MIT using their ARPANET accounts.

106 *A practical guide to using software usability labs: lessons learned at IBM*, Janet L Fath, Teresa L Mann and Thomas G Holzman, Behaviour and Information Technology, Vol 13, 1994.

107 *Human Factors In Engineering and Design*, Mark S Sanders and Ernest J McCormick, McGraw-Hill Science, 1993.

108 easyJet were recently in the news for turning away an already seated unaccompanied minor when it transpired someone else had the same seat number for the flight. In the wake of a much worse US Airlines example a few months earlier, this became headline news. It was an issue that was exacerbated by the airline's adoption in 2012 of what would once have been seen as heresy for a low-cost airline, allocated seating. See *easyJet comes under fire for removing unaccompanied minor from flight*, Helen Coffey, Independent, 21 July 2017 et al.

109 Said by Walter White (Bryan Cranston) in *Breaking Bad*, Season 5 Episode 6, Netflix.

110 Amazon ROI, Investopedia, 26/05/2017.

111 *Is Amazon Finally Focussing on Profitability?* Forbes, 11/07/2016.

112 *No Big Deal: Why Michael Dell Isn't Afraid of The New Compaq*, D Kirkpatrick, Fortune Magazine, 02/03/1998.

113 Chrysler was worth $36 billion at the time of the merger, and was sold to venture capitalist Cerberus for $7.4 billion 9 years later.

114 *Taken For A Ride: How Daimler-Benz Drove Off With Chrysler*, B Vlasic and BA Stertz, Wiley, 2000.

115 Reported in ComputerWorld, 26/06/2016.

116 *Microsoft Forms a Patent Bloc With Apple, EMC, and Oracle*, E Sherman, CBS moneywatch, 16/12/2010 and *Just What's Inside Microsoft's New Stash of Novell Patents?* E Sherman, CBS moneywatch, 22/11/2010.

117 *Fad Surfing in the Boardroom*, Eileen C Shapiro, Basic Books, 1996.

118 *The New New Thing: A Silicon Valley Story,* Michael Lewis, Hodder, 2000.

119 *Stop Focussing on Your Core Business*, A Hartung, Forbes, 27/07/2010.

120 The 1964 Resale Prices Act outlawed supplier-controlled prices ('manufacturers recommended prices') and allowed retailers to charge whatever they liked. Comet, operating mainly as a mail-order retailer, but also allowing customers to buy from what were, in effect, simply their warehouses, was able to undercut many of the traditional high-street companies, Dixons included, creating a downward spiral in prices from which arguably they never recovered.

The Wedding Planner

121 As at August 2017.

122 Compass Group Annual Report 2016.

123 A notable exception is the Patina Group, an American subsidiary which was acquired as part of Restaurant Associates in 1993, and which has some very nice upmarket restaurants in New York, including Brasserie 8½ on Fifth Avenue and Nick and Stef's Steakhouse on Pennsylvania Plaza.

124 Compass Group later sold off its travel concessions business, SSP, to a private equity consortium for £1.8 billion in 2006.

125 The most famous recent subsidy-type contact win being the staff canteen at Google, which is free to its employees.

126 These last contract types, especially 'cost-plus', are becoming increasingly less common as clients become smarter at buying in food services (often advised by ex-contract caterers turned purchasing consultants about what the 'costs' might actually consist of) and the eating habits of employees change.

127 Following on from the discussion in the previous chapter, a very rare example of a UK company acquiring a French one, or at least a French-based subsidiary of one.

128 An acronym which it doesn't help to explain. OK then, it stands for *Systeme, Anwendungen und Produkte in der Datenverarbeitung*; or *Systems, Applications and Products in Data Processing* in English. Told you so.

129 The other being Oracle. Most large companies at the time (and indeed since) who have wanted to deploy multi-national, enterprise-wide integrated systems have been faced with the task of choosing between these two behemoths, and

the reasons given (both by the software company's pre-sales team and, in post-justification mode, by the organisations which have made the choice) make interesting, but for the second reason, not very instructive reading. See the discussion in the Lesson 3 section of this chapter for the approach which should always be taken.

130 It is interesting to compare this amount with the spending of other leading software development companies: e.g. IBM spends $4.8 billion a year on R&D, while Microsoft spends upward of $14 billion, about half of its total cost base (although critics would argue that it is mainly on D rather than R). You can use that figure if anyone complains that MS Office is too expensive at $200. Figures from company reports via ycharts.com

131 ReMACS was later acquired by Radiant Systems of Atlanta in 1997, who were then subsequently acquired in 2011 by NCR: with a R&D budget of over $200 million a year, proving that for success in the world of international systems, scale matters.

132 Those assets consisted of, for Compass Group, its UK operations in Business and Industry catering (Eurest, Roux Fine Dining and the like), the SSP concessions business, plus numerous client facing brands in the hospitality, hospitals and schools feeding sectors; and for Granada, its extensive media interests, its hotels, plus the catering businesses which included 75% of all motorway service stations as well as the Sutcliffe's Business and Industry division.

133 Granada Media subsequently merged with Carlton Communications in 2003 to create ITV plc.

134 The hotels were major assets, including the Posthouse,

Méridien, Heritage and Signature chains, the sale of which fetched nearly £4 billion.

135 FRS – Financial Reporting Standards, the equivalent of Statutory Guidance for company accountants, are issued by the Financial Reporting Council, who are tasked with, as well as issuing guidance on reporting, overseeing corporate governance and good stewardship, also regulate the actuarial and accountancy professions. Their work can be viewed at www.frc.org.uk.

136 *See Similarities and Differences: A comparison of IFRS, US GAAP and UK GAAP*, PriceWatersCoopers, 2005. Compulsory reading for any chronic insomniac.

137 In 1999, Matthews was subsequently overlooked for the top job (and left the company without another role to go to), in favour of Mike Bailey who had previously been CEO of the North American division. It is possible that the stylistic differences which were exposed during the implementation of the strategic review (which Matthews had led) might have had something to do with this decision. *Matthews Loses Top Compass Job to Bailey*, David Shrimpton, The Caterer, 01/07/1999.

138 My induction in week one consisted of a flight from London to Boston (I forget why there particularly) for a two-day strategy review meeting, followed by a flight to San Francisco in order to visit ReMACS in Pleasanton (fittingly, given the little town's name, a very pleasant experience; not least for the kind hospitality of Dave Douglas, the CEO, and the wonderful discovery of Retzlaff wines) followed by a red-eye to Charlotte, NC and three days later another overnighter back to the UK. Looking back, I assume it was a test, which

I think I failed through the indulgence of taking a business-class seat back to the UK in the hope of getting at least some sleep before I went straight into the office the next morning (all the other legs were economy), but anyway, I was too jet-lagged to care.

139 There are many guides about how to implement SAP (but very few on the long-term implications of the decisions which need to be taken). See for example *Successful SAP R/3 Implementation*, Norbert Welti, Addison-Wesley Longman Publishing, 1999

140 *Firms Need a BluePrint for Building their IT Systems*, Donald A Marchand and Joe Peppard, Harvard Business Review, 18/06/2015

141 *Competitive Strategy: Techniques for Analysing Industries and Competitors*, Michael E Porter, Free Press, 1998

142 A very personal and frustrating example I experienced while writing this, when I had to break off from deep concentration to ring our insurer, Hiscox, to renew our house contents policy.

143 *Uber drivers win UK legal battle for workers' rights*, Jane Croft and Madhumita Murgia, Financial Times, 28/10/2016.

144 One benefit of working for a foodservice company is that you do eat well! The corporate head office in Chertsey had the luxury of a resident executive chef from Roux Fine Dining, part of the UK business. There to impress visiting VIPs such as investors, analysts, clients and the occasional acquisition target, at other times he was relegated to providing lunch on a daily basis for other, mere mortals such as myself, who were based there. I did however get to eat some of the best cheese and ham sandwiches I've ever tasted, although I suspect he

probably described them as *bleu des Causses et jambon fumé sur un petit pain*.

145 *How the Dollar Store Was Won*, S Tully, Fortune Magazine, 24/04/2017 is an entertaining read about how the deal was done.

146 *The High Price of Dollar Stores*, J Pillar and JS Strong, Babson College Publications, 2015.

147 In the six months which the review took, 99p Stores lost its credit insurance, which meant that many suppliers would not trade with it.

148 Poundland Annual Report. July 2016.

149 *Co-Op Bank hits out at Capita in row over mortgage contract, Rhiannon Bury and Kate Palmer*, The Telegraph, 29/09/2016. As a result of this dispute and risk of litigation, Capita reported pre-tax profits down by 50%, resulting in a one-day fall of 27% in the share price.

150 Compass Group no longer reports UK numbers separately – Europe was 28% of its 2015–2016 turnover.

151 *Capita boss exits as profits plunge at beleaguered outsourcer*, Sam Dean and Rhiannon Bury, The Telegraph, 02/03/2017.

152 One of the most transformational changes in the employee feeding marketplace took place in the late 1990s at IBM, when, in order to keep on-site employees who had started leaving their factories at lunchtime to visit, for example, a Burger King at a local shopping mall, IBM was encouraged by Compass Group North America to let them build a similar type of food plaza in a part of their factory. This was made to look and feel almost identical to the one down the road, with a selection of different food outlets (all of course run by Compass Group), set in a pleasant environment with indoor

plants, comfortable seating and nice background music. The innovation was that, as well as massively increasing the number of employees who stayed on-site to eat (creating a hard-to-measure but noticeable productivity improvement), it turned what had been the traditional employee feeding business model on its head: instead of IBM paying Compass to run the facility in the form of a subsidy, Compass Group started paying IBM a concession fee to operate there. The benefit to IBM was considerable on both fronts, and (despite the new concession fee and lack of subsidy income) Compass Group also increased *its* profits by the simple expedient of now being able to charge the employees three times as much for the same portion of fries, the only difference in the actual product being that the carton in which the fries were served now had the words 'Burger King' written on the side. The authors of *Freakonomics*, Steven Levitt and Stephen J Dubner, (see Laura Ashley case study Notes) would have been proud.

153 Some contracts can be extremely complex, such as the one run by Eurest for client BAA at Heathrow, which offers food to all of the 75,000 people who work in some capacity within the airport boundary. They work for many different companies, each of which might want a completely different pricing or discount structure for their own employees.

154 That very useful French phrase again.

155 This problem is covered in great depth in a book which has been mentioned before in the Introduction, *The E-Myth: Why Most Businesses Don't Work and What to Do About It*, Michael E Gerber, Ballinger Publishing, 1986.

156 There was a similar story which Ryanair ensured was well publicised, which was that Michael O'Leary, its brash, larger-

than-life and publicity-savvy head, had banned staff from charging their own mobile phones in the office in order to save money. Again, whether this was true or not (it almost certainly wasn't, at least apart from that week), it nevertheless created a splash in the press and reinforced in people's minds that Ryanair was passionate about being low-cost (or, expressed in terms which even Michael O'Leary would have been secretly delighted with, tight). See for example *Ryanair's latest cut on costs: staff banned from charging phones*, Andrew Clark (who, like everyone else, fell for it), The Guardian, 23/04/2005.

157 See *Simplicity-Minded Management*, Ron Ashkenas, Harvard Business Review, December 2007, and his book, *Simply Effective: How to Cut Through Complexity in Your Organization and Get Things Done*, Harvard Business Press, 2009. He also wrote an excellent book, *The GE Workout*, McGraw-Hill, 2002, which builds on the Jack Welsh approach to solving business problems.

158 *Knowledge Links: How Firms Compete Through Strategic Alliances*, Joseph L Badaracco, Harvard Business Publishing, 1991

159 The other great story allegedly concerns the first shipment of parts from Japan into the Nummi facility: when they arrived, taped to the top of the box of 1000 components was apparently a small packet containing one extra part. A note attached to it explained that, as the Japanese plant which had manufactured them had not understood the American quality standard which allowed for one defective part per 1000, they had taken the liberty of enclosing a defective one separately to avoid any confusion.

160 *Executing Your Business Transformation: How to Engage*

Sweeping Change without Killing Yourself or your Business, Mark Morgan, Andrew Cole, Dave Johnson and Rob Johnson, Wiley, 2010.

161 Sorry, I promised I wouldn't mention another merger – last one.

162 *15 years later: lessons from the failed AOL-Time Warner merger*, Rita G McGrath, Fortune Magazine, 10/01/2015.

163 Reported in Wall Street Journal, 30/01/2003.

164 The most famous book on this topic is *The Fifth Discipline: The art and practice of the learning organisation*, Peter M Senge, Random House, 2006.

165 *Marketing, 4th Edition*, P Baines, C Fill and S Rosengren, OUP, 2017.

166 *An Introduction to European Intergovernmental Organisations*, M Cogen, Routledge, 2016

167 The aircraft 'options' were what is known as 'Purchasing Options', a looser commitment than 'Booked Options', which guarantee a production slot. It just means that the buyer has committed to the price for that particular aircraft without any dates, and which can later, as easyJet subsequently did several times, be traded in or changed for other aircraft at order time.

168 *EasyJet snubs Boeing and turns to Airbus*, Susie Mesure, The Independent, 14/10/2002.

169 easyJet makes 20% of its income from what it calls 'ancillary revenue', about 45% of which is from checked baggage, but about 8% of the 20% comes from on-board sales of food and merchandise, which doesn't directly rely on real-time systems availability, even for credit card processing, so, assuming the flight can actually take off before the systems fail, sales can still be made. Source *easyJet annual report*, 2016.

170 See *British Airways system outage 'caused by IT worker accidentally switching off the power supply'*, Josie Cox, Independent, 02/06/2017 et al. Really??

171 easyJet was able to be specific about its future passenger numbers, which were forecast at the time to grow at 7.5–10% pa, because of its future pipeline of incoming Airbus orders, which it had to fly. Locking in a future (and falling) cost per seat for its IT systems gave certainty in at least one, albeit very small, cost area, in a world where fluctuations in the price of fuel and foreign exchange can make the biggest difference.

172 *easyJet signs 5 year outsourcing deal*, 26/10/2006, retrieved from www.bcs.org.

173 At the time, if IBM's mid-range AS/400 business had been separated out from IBM, it would have been, by far, the second largest computer business in the world; second, that is, only to the rest of IBM.

174 It is very hard nowadays (in a world where it is possible to buy a 2-terabyte PC external hard drive for £50) to properly quantify this order. In 1992, an IBM AS/400 9337-040 disk array with a capacity of just under 8 gigabytes had a list price of $62,000, and The Burton Group needed to acquire 64gb of new data storage to support IFPR and mirroring. If nothing had changed in the price of disks (and the sterling/US dollar exchange rate is about the same at the time of writing as it was in the early 1990s) that 2-terabyte hard drive would today have cost you, not £50, but £12 million; a perfect (and mathematically precise) example of Moore's Law. See *Moore's Law: The Life of Gordon Moore, Silicon Valley's Quiet Revolutionary*, Arnold Thackray, David Brock and Rachel Jones, Basic Books, 2015, for details of this and much more.

175 If you drive into London from the west, off the M40 and down the elevated section of the Westway, you will see on your left-hand side the old Data General building, constructed in the 1990s shortly before the company's demise. It is easily recognisable, as the letters D and G are proudly woven into the shape of the windows; a poignant and permanent monument to corporate vanity.

176 2005 was to be CEO Mike Bailey's last year of office, and was notable for the issue of three profit warnings (never since repeated) and the scandal surrounding the award of United Nations contracts which led to the dismissal of three UK executives. See *Rival Claimed Caterer Bribed its Way to Commercial Success*, Salamander Davoudi, Financial Times, 20/03/2006 and *Compass Settles UN Bribery Case for £40m*, Philip Aldrick, The Telegraph, 16/10/2006. Shortly afterwards, Sir Francis Mackay (Chairman and the original architect, alongside Gerry Robinson and Charles Allen, of both the management buyout from Grand Metropolitan in 1987 and the Granada merger in 2000), also retired.

177 *Expanding Fast in All Directions*, Financial Times, 15/08/1999

178 While this book was being prepared for publication, Richard Cousins and his family were tragically killed in a plane crash on New Year's Eve 2017 near Sydney, Australia. The company had only recently announced his retirement and replacement by Dominic Blakemore, previously COO for Europe. A sad end to a distinguished career. *Compass Group Richard Cousins killed in aircraft crash*, Mark Wembridge, Financial Times, 01/01/2018.

179 *The Best-Performing CEOs in the World*, Harvard Business Review, November 2014 and November 2016.

The Final Cut

180 Quoted in *The Ghost in the Machine*, Arthur Koestler, Hutchinson, 1967.